The experience that counts!

The experience that counts!

or

Spiritual experience, true or false?

An abridged version, re-written for today's readers, of the classic 'A treatise concerning religious affections' by Jonathan Edwards, A.M. (1703-58)

The full work is available with The Banner of Truth Trust, Edinburgh, EH12 6EL.

Prepared by Dr. N. R. Needham, B.D., PhD.

Grace Publications Trust

Joint managing editors J. P. Arthur, M.A.
H. J. Appleby

139 Grosvenor Avenue
LONDON N5 2NH
England
1991

British library cataloguing in publication data

ISBN 0946462 23 2

Distributed by:
EVANGELICAL PRESS
12 Wooler Street
Darlington
Co. Durham
DL1 1RQ

Cover design by: Peter Smith

Printed by: Cox & Wyman, Reading, England.

Contents

Introduction

Jonathan Edwards (1703-58), America's greatest theologian, wrote his **Treatise concerning religious affections** against the background of the First Great Awakening, the American equivalent of what the British call the Evangelical Revival. Edwards himself played a prominent part in the Awakening as pastor of a Congregational church in Northampton, Massachusetts.

Edwards' desire to distinguish between true and false religious experience arose out of his pastoral concern in the context of revival. He preached a series of sermons on 1 Peter 1:8 dealing with this subject in 1742-3. The **Treatise** was the text of these sermons revised for publication in 1746.

Edwards had to fight on two fronts. On the one hand, he had to argue against those who dismissed the entire revival as mindless hysteria. On the other hand, he had to argue against those who seemed to think everything that happened in the revival was 'of God', no matter how strange, wild or unbalanced it was. Do these two opposite reactions sound familiar?

In his attempt to chart a middle path between these equal and opposite extremes, Edwards confronted a series of fundamental questions. What does it mean to be a Christian? Is Christianity a matter of the intellect alone? What about desires, feelings, and experiences? What is conversion? How do we know that people have been converted? How far should we go in testing an apparent conversion to see if it is real? What place does assurance of salvation have in Christian experience? Which religious experiences should we encourage, and which should we discourage? How can we test the sincerity and reality of our own faith? What are the signs of religious hypocrisy and delusion?

We may not be living in the midst of a revival, but these questions, and the answers Edwards gives to them, are profoundly relevant to us today. Feelings and experiences have perhaps never been emphasised so strongly and sought so eagerly as they are among Christians in our generation. The results have too often been unbalanced, undiscerning and spiritually harmful. Reacting against this, others have retreated into a hard, cold, dry orthodoxy, looking with deep suspicion on anything 'emotional'.

In Edwards we will find 'a guide for the perplexed' — a voice of clear Biblical and spiritual sanity to lead us safely through the maze of contemporary confusion in this crucial area.

A note on 'Affections' and 'Emotions'

The word 'affections' appears in the original title of Edwards' book and throughout its pages. To us today, 'affection' means a certain kind of love. In Edwards' day, however, it had a far wider meaning. So I have decided to modernise the word as 'emotions', which seems the best modern equivalent of what Edwards meant by 'affections'.

The Oxford English Dictionary lists thirteen definitions of 'affection'. The second and fifth show us what Edwards had in mind when he used the word: 'an emotion, or feeling'; 'state of mind towards a thing; disposition towards'.

'Emotions' for Edwards were movements of the will. In fact, in Part One, chapter 2, Edwards clearly defines emotions as the more vivid, powerful and lively movements of the will. With our intellect or reason, we 'see' things; with our will, we like or dislike what we see. So 'emotion' always involves both the intellect and the will. It simply means (for Edwards) a strong response of the will to what the intellect sees — whether that response is desire, hope, joy, love, zeal, pity, grief, fear, anger or hatred.

Edwards called these strong responses of the will 'affections'. I have called them 'emotions'. As long as we bear in mind the realities Edwards was talking about, it does not greatly matter what we call them. But because of the rather narrow meaning that 'affection' has gained in popular speech today, it seemed less misleading to drop the term and employ 'emotion' instead. Wherever the word 'affection' does appear in this abridged version, it has its modern meaning of 'love'.

(All Biblical quotations are from the Revised Authorised Version unless otherwise stated. NASB = New American Standard Bible.)

N.R.N.
Edinburgh 1991

Preface

The most crucial question for the human race, and for every individual person, is this: **What are the distinguishing marks of the people who enjoy God's favour — those who are on their way to heaven?** This is just another way of asking: **What is the nature of true religion? What sort of personal religion does God approve of?**

It is hard to give an objective answer to such a controversial question. It is even harder to **write** about it objectively. And it is hardest of all to **read** about it objectively! It will probably hurt many of my readers to find that I have criticised so many religious emotions and experiences in this book. On the other hand, others may be angry about the things I have defended and approved. I have tried to be balanced. It is not easy to support what is good in religious revivals, and at the same time to see and reject what is bad in them. Yet surely we have to do both, if we want Christ's kingdom to prosper.

There is something very mysterious about it, I admit. So much good and so much bad are mixed up in the Church! It is as mysterious as the mixture of so much good and bad in an individual Christian. Still, neither of these mysteries is new. It is no new thing for false religion to flourish at a time of revival, or for hypocrites to appear among true believers. This happened in that great revival in Josiah's time, as we see from Jeremiah 3:10 and 4:3-4. It was the same in the days of John the Baptist. John aroused all Israel by his preaching, and yet most fell away soon afterwards. John 5:35 — 'you were willing for a time to rejoice in his light.' It was the same again when Christ himself preached. Many admired Christ for a time, but few were faithful to the end. And the same was true again when the apostles preached, as we know from the heresies and divisions that troubled the churches during the apostles' lifetime.

This mixture of false religion with true has been Satan's greatest weapon against the cause of Christ. This is why we **must** learn to distinguish between true and false religion — between emotions and experiences which really come from salvation, and imitations which are outwardly attractive and plausible, but false.

A failure to distinguish between true and false religion produces terrible consequences. For example:

(i) Many offer to God a false worship which they think is acceptable to him, but which he rejects.

(ii) Satan deceives many about the state of their souls. In this way he eternally ruins them. In some cases, Satan deludes people into thinking they are outstandingly holy, when really they are the worst hypocrites.

(iii) Satan spoils the faith of true believers. He mixes deformities and corruptions into it, and so causes believers to grow cold in their spiritual emotions. He also confuses others with great difficulties and temptations.

(iv) The outright enemies of Christianity are encouraged, when they see the Church so corrupted and distracted.

(v) Men commit sin under the illusion that they are serving God. So they sin without restraint.

(vi) False teaching deceives even the friends of Christianity into doing, without realising it, the work of its enemies. They destroy Christianity far more effectively than outright enemies can do, under the illusion that they are advancing it.

(vii) Satan divides Christ's people and sets them against each other. Christians quarrel with great heat as if this were spiritual zeal. Christianity degenerates into empty disputes. The quarrelling parties rush off into opposite extremes, until the right path in the middle becomes almost totally neglected.

When Christians see the terrible consequences of false religion passing for true religion, it unsettles their minds. They do not know where to turn or what to think. Many doubt whether there is anything real in Christianity at all. Heresy, unbelief and atheism begin to spread.

For these reasons, it is vital that we should do all we can to understand the nature of true religion. Until we do this, we cannot expect revivals to last long, and we can expect little good from our religious discussions and debates, since we will not even know what we are arguing for!

My plan is to contribute what I can in this book to an understanding of true religion. I aim to show the nature and signs of the Holy Spirit's work in converting sinners. I will also try to show how we can distinguish the Spirit's work from everything which is not a true experience of salvation. If I succeed, I hope this book will help to promote the interests of genuine Christianity.

May God accept the sincerity of my efforts, and may the true followers of the meek and loving Lamb of God accept my offering with open minds and with prayer!

Jonathan Edwards

Part One.
The nature of emotions and their importance in Christianity.

1.
Opening remarks about emotions.

The apostle Peter says of the relationship between Christians and Christ: 'though you have not seen him, you love him, and though you do not see him now, but believe in him, you greatly rejoice with joy inexpressible and full of glory' (1 Peter 1:8, NASB).

As the previous verses make clear, the believers to whom Peter wrote were suffering persecution. Here he observes how their Christianity affected them during these persecutions. He mentions two clear signs that their Christianity was genuine:

(i) **Love for Christ.** 'Though you have not seen him, you love him.' Non-Christians were amazed that Christians were ready to expose themselves to such sufferings, and to forsake the joys and comforts of this world. These Christians seemed mad to their unbelieving neighbours. They seemed to act as if they hated themselves. Unbelievers saw nothing which could inspire them to suffer like this. Indeed, the Christians saw nothing with their bodily eyes. They loved someone whom they could not see! They loved Jesus Christ, for they saw him spiritually, even though they could not see him physically.

(ii) **Joy in Christ.** Though their outward sufferings were terrible, their inward spiritual joys were greater than their sufferings. These joys strengthened them and enabled them to suffer cheerfully.

Peter notes two things about this joy. First, he tells us its origin. It came from faith. 'Though you do not see him now, but believe in him, you greatly rejoice.'

Second, he describes the nature of this joy: 'inexpressible and full of glory'. It was inexpressible joy, because it was so different from the joys of the world. It was pure and heavenly. There were no words to describe its excellence and sweetness. It was also inexpressible in its extent, because God had so freely poured out this joy on his suffering people.

Then Peter describes this joy as being 'full of glory'. This joy filled the minds of the Christians, as it were, with a glorious brightness. It did not corrupt the mind, as many worldly joys do, but gave it glory and dignity. The suffering Christians were sharing in the joy of heaven. This joy filled their minds with the light of God's glory, and made them shine with that glory.

Now, the doctrine Peter is teaching us is this: TRUE RELIGION CONSISTS MAINLY IN HOLY EMOTIONS. (See the special note on EMOTIONS in the Introduction — N.R.N.)

Peter singles out the spiritual emotions of love and joy when he describes the experience of these Christians. Remember, he is speaking about believers who were suffering persecution. Their sufferings were purifying their faith, causing it 'to result in praise and glory and honour at the revelation of Jesus Christ' (v.7 NASB). Thus they were in a spiritually healthy condition, and Peter highlights their love and joy as evidences of their spiritual health.

2.
What are emotions?

At this point, it might be asked: 'What exactly do you mean when you speak about emotions?'

I answer as follows: 'Emotions are the more lively and intense actions of the soul's inclination and will.'

God has given the human soul two main powers. The first is **understanding**, by which we examine and judge things. The second power enables us to look at things, not as indifferent spectators, but as liking or disliking them, pleased or displeased by them, approving or rejecting them. We sometimes call this second power our **inclination**. In its relationship to our decisions, we usually call it **the will**. When the mind exercises its inclination or will, then we often call the mind '**the heart**'.

Human beings act by their wills in two ways. (i) We can move **towards** the things we see, by liking them and approving of them. (ii) We can turn **away** from the things we see, and reject them. These acts of the will, of course, differ greatly in degree. There are some inclinations of like or dislike which move us only slightly beyond total apathy. There are other degrees in which the like or dislike is stronger, until the strength is so great that we act in an energetic, deliberate way.

It is these more energetic and intense acts of the will which we call 'emotions'.

Our will and our emotions are not two different things. Our emotions differ from casual acts of choice only in their energy and vividness. However, I admit that language can express only an imperfect sense of this difference. In one sense, the emotions of the soul are the same as its will, and the will never moves from a state of apathy unless it feels. Yet there are many acts of the will which we do not call 'emotions'. The difference is not a difference in nature, but in the strength of activity and the way the will acts.

In every act of will, we either like or dislike what we see. Our liking for something, if it is vigorous and lively, is the very same thing as the emotion of **love**; and an equally strong dislike is the same as **hatred**. In every act of will for or towards something, we are in some degree **inclined** to that thing; and if this inclination is strong, we call it **desire**. In every act of will in which we approve of something, there is a degree of pleasure; and if the pleasure is great, we call it **joy** or **delight**. And if our will disapproves of something, we are in some degree displeased; if the displeasure is great, we call it **grief** or **sorrow**.

Every act of will is concerned either with approving and liking, or else with disapproving and rejecting. So our emotions are of two kinds. There are emotions which carry us **towards** what we see, clinging to it or seeking it. These emotions include **love, desire, hope, joy, gratitude**, and **pleasure**. Then there are emotions which turn us away from what we see, opposing it. These include **hatred, fear, anger** and **grief**.

3.
True religion consists mainly in emotions.

Who can deny that true religion consists mainly in emotions — in vigorous and energetic actions of the will? The religion which God requires does not consist in weak, dull and lifeless wishes, raising us only a little above apathy. In his word, God greatly insists that we be serious, spiritually energetic, and our hearts vigorously involved in Christianity. We must be 'fervent in spirit, serving the Lord' (Romans 12:11). 'And now, O Israel, what does the Lord your God require of you, but to fear the Lord your God, to walk in all his ways and to love him, to serve the Lord your God with all your heart and with all your soul?' (Deuteronomy 10:12). 'Hear, O Israel: the Lord our God, the Lord is one! You shall love the Lord your God with all your heart, with all your soul, and with all your might' (Deuteronomy 6:4-5).

This lively, vigorous involvement of the heart in true religion is the result of a spiritual circumcision, or regeneration, to which the promises of life belong. 'And the Lord your God will circumcise your heart and the heart of your descendants, to love the Lord your God with all your heart and with all your soul, that you may live' (Deuteronomy 30:6).

If we are not serious in our Christianity, and our wills are not vigorously active, we are nothing. Spiritual realities are so great, that our hearts do not respond suitably to them unless they act energetically and powerfully. In nothing is the exertion of our wills so necessary as in spiritual things; in nothing is lukewarmness so hateful. True religion is powerful, and its power first appears in the heart. This is why Scripture calls true religion 'the power of godliness', as distinct from outward appearances which are only its form — 'having a form of godliness, but denying its power' (2 Timothy 3:5). The Holy Spirit is a Spirit of powerful holy emotion in real Christians. This is why Scripture says that God has given us a spirit 'of power and of love and of a sound mind' (2 Timothy 1:7). When we receive the Holy Spirit, Scripture says that we are baptized 'with the Holy Spirit and fire' (Matthew 3:11). This 'fire' represents the holy emotions which the Spirit produces in us, so that our hearts 'burn within us' (Luke 24:32).

Sometimes Scripture makes a comparison between our relationship to spiritual things and those activities which men vigorously perform in secular affairs. Examples are running (1 Corinthians 9:24), wrestling (Ephesians 6:12), agonising for a prize (Revelation 2:10), fighting with strong enemies (1 Peter 5:8-9), and full-scale war (1 Timothy 1:18). Grace, of course, has degrees, and there are weak Christians in whom the acts of the will towards spiritual things are comparatively feeble. However, every true Christian's emotions towards God are stronger than his natural or sinful emotions. Every genuine disciple of Christ loves him above 'father and mother, wife and children, brothers and sisters, yes, and his own life also' (Luke 14:26).

God who created us has not only given us emotions, but has made them very much the cause of our actions. We do not make decisions or act, unless love, hate, desire, hope, fear, or some other emotion, influences us. This applies in both secular and spiritual affairs. It is why many people hear God's Word telling them about infinitely important things — about God and Christ, sin and salvation, heaven and hell — and yet it makes no change in their attitude or behaviour. The reason is simple: what they hear does not affect them. **It does not touch their emotions.** Indeed, I boldly claim that no spiritual truth ever changed a person's attitude or conduct, unless it aroused his emotions. No sinner ever hungered for salvation, no Christian ever awoke from spiritual coldness, unless the truth affected his heart. The emotions are as important as that!

4. The different emotions.

Scripture everywhere places true religion mainly in our emotions — in fear, hope, love, hatred, desire, joy, sorrow, gratitude, compassion and zeal. Let us consider these for a moment.

Fear. Scripture makes godly fear a chief part of true religion. A name which Scripture often gives to believers is 'fearers of God', or those 'who fear the Lord'. This is why true godliness is commonly called 'the fear of God'.

Hope. Hope in God and in his promises is, according to Scripture, an important part of true religion. The apostle Paul mentions hope as one of the three great things which make up true religion (1 Corinthians 13:13). Hope is the helmet of the Christian soldier: 'And as a helmet the hope of salvation' (1 Thessalonians 5:8). It is the anchor of the soul: 'This hope we have as an anchor of the soul, both sure and steadfast' (Hebrews 6:19). Sometimes godly fear and hope are joined together as defining the character of the true believer: 'Behold, the eye of the Lord is on those who fear him, on those who hope in his mercy' (Psalm 33:18).

Love. Scripture places true religion very much in the emotion of love: love for God, for Jesus Christ, for God's people, and for mankind. The verses which teach this are countless, and I will deal with this in my next chapter. We should observe, though, that Scripture speaks of the opposite emotion of hatred — the hatred of sin — as an important part of true religion. 'The fear of the Lord is to hate evil' (Proverbs 8:13). Accordingly Scripture calls upon believers to prove their sincerity by this: 'You who love the Lord, hate evil!' (Psalm 97:10).

Desire. Scripture often mentions holy desire, expressed in longings, hungerings and thirstings after God and holiness, as an important part of true religion. 'The desire of our soul is for your name' (Isaiah 26:8). 'My soul thirsts for you, my flesh longs for you, in a dry and thirsty land where there is no water' (Psalm 63:1-2). 'Blessed are those who hunger and thirst for righteousness, for they shall be filled' (Matthew 5:6).

Joy. Scripture speaks of joy as a great part of true religion. 'Rejoice in the Lord, you righteous' (Psalm 97:12). 'Rejoice in the Lord always. Again I will say, rejoice!' (Philippians 4:4). 'The fruit of the Spirit is love, joy,' etc. (Galatians 5:22).

Sorrow. Spiritual sorrow, contrition, and brokenness of heart, are a great part of true religion, according to Scripture. 'Blessed are those who mourn, for they shall be comforted' (Matthew 5:4). 'The sacrifices of God are a broken spirit, a broken and a contrite heart — these, O God, you will not despise' (Psalm 51:17). 'For thus says the high and lofty one who inhabits eternity, whose name is holy: "I dwell in the high and holy place, with him who has a contrite and humble spirit, to revive the spirit of the humble and to revive the heart of the contrite ones"' (Isaiah 57:15).

Gratitude. Another spiritual emotion Scripture often mentions is gratitude, especially as expressed in the praise of God. This appears so often, especially in the Psalms, that I need not mention particular texts.

Mercy. Scripture frequently speaks of compassion or mercy as an essential thing in true religion. Jesus taught that mercy is one of the most important demands of God's law: 'Blessed are the merciful, for they shall obtain mercy' (Matthew 5:7). 'Woe to you, scribes and Pharisees, hypocrites! For you pay the tithe of mint and anise and cumin, and have neglected the weightier matters of the law: justice and mercy and faith' (Matthew 23:23). Paul emphasised this virtue as much as Jesus did: 'Therefore, as the elect of God, holy and beloved, put on tender mercies' (Colossians 3:12).

Zeal. Scripture says that spiritual zeal is an essential part of true religion. Christ had the production of this quality in mind when he died for us: 'who gave himself for us, that he might redeem us from every lawless deed and purify for himself his own special people, zealous for good works' (Titus 2:14).

I have mentioned just a few texts out of a great number which place true religion very much in our emotions. If anyone wishes to dispute this, he must throw away the Bible and find some other standard by which to judge the nature of true religion.

5.
True religion is summed up in love.

Love is the chief of all the emotions. This is what Jesus taught when someone asked him what the greatest commandment was: 'You shall love the Lord your God with all your heart, with all your soul, and with all your mind. This is the first and great commandment. And the second is like it: You shall love your neighbour as yourself. On these two commandments hang all the Law and the Prophets' (Matthew 22:37-40).

The apostle Paul taught the same: 'love is the fulfilment of the law' (Romans 13:10). 'The purpose of the commandment is love from a pure heart' (1 Timothy 1:5). In 1 Corinthians 13 Paul speaks of love as the greatest thing in Christianity, the essence and soul of it, without which the greatest knowledge and gifts and actions are all worthless.

This clearly proves that true religion lies mainly in our emotions. For love is not just one of the emotions, but the chief of them and (so to speak) the fountain of the others. It is from love that hatred arises — hatred of the things which are contrary to what we love. From a vigorous, affectionate, and fervent love of God, will arise the other spiritual emotions: a hatred of sin; a fear of displeasing God; gratitude to God for his goodness; joy in God when we experience his presence; sorrow when we feel his absence; hope for a future enjoyment of God; zeal for God's glory. In the same way, love for our fellow men will produce every other right feeling towards them.

6.
David, Paul, John and Christ as examples of holy emotion.

The religion of the most outstanding saints in Scripture was a religion of holy emotions. I shall take particular notice of three great saints, and of their Master himself, to show the truth of this.

First, we will consider King David, that man after God's own heart, who has left us a lively portrait of his religion in the Psalms. Those holy songs are nothing else but the outpourings of devout and holy emotion. In them we see a humble and fervent love of God, admiration of his glorious perfections and wonderful works, and desires and thirstings of the soul towards him. We see delight and happiness in God, a sweet and melting gratitude for his great goodness, and a holy rejoicing in his favour, sufficiency and faithfulness. We see love for and delight in God's people, great delight in God's Word and ordinances, sorrow for David's own sins and the sins of others, and fervent zeal for God and against God's enemies.

These expressions of holy emotion in the Psalms are especially relevant to us. The Psalms not only express the religion of so great a saint as King David, but the Holy Spirit also inspired them for believers to sing in public worship, in David's time and ever afterwards.

Next, let us consider the apostle Paul. By what Scripture says of him, he appears to have been a man with a highly developed emotional life, especially where love was concerned. This is clear from Paul's letters. A most ardent love for Christ seems to set him on fire and swallow him up. He pictures himself as overpowered by this holy emotion, compelled by it to go forward in his ministry through all difficulties and sufferings (2 Corinthians 5:14-15). And his letters are full of an overflowing love for Christians. He calls them his beloved ones (2 Corinthians 12:19, Philippians 4:1, 2 Timothy 1:2), and speaks of his affectionate and tender care towards them (1 Thessalonians 2:7-8). He frequently speaks of his affectionate and longing desires for them (Romans 1:11, Philippians 1:8, 1 Thessalonians 2:8, 2 Timothy 1:4).

Paul often expresses the emotion of joy. He speaks of his rejoicing with great joy (Philippians 4:10, Philemon 7), of his rejoicing exceedingly (2 Corinthians 7:13), and always rejoicing (2 Corinthians 6:10). See also 2 Corinthians 1:12, 7:7, 9, 16; Philippians 1:4, 2:1-2, 3:3; Colossians 1:24; 1 Thessalonians 3:9. He also speaks of his hope (Philippians 1:20), his godly jealousy (2 Corinthians 11:2-3), and his sorrowful tears (Acts 20:19,31, and 2 Corinthians 2:4). He writes of the great and continual sorrow in his heart because of the unbelief of the Jews (Romans 9:2). And I need not mention his spiritual zeal, which is obvious from his entire life as Christ's apostle.

If anyone can consider these Scriptural accounts of Paul, and not see that Paul's religion was a religion of emotion, he must have a strange ability to shut his eyes to the light shining full in his face!

The apostle John was a man of the same type. It is clear from all his writings that he was a person with a profound emotional life. He addresses the Christians to whom he wrote in an extremely touching and tender way. His letters breathe nothing but the most fervent love, as though he were made of sweet and holy affection. I cannot really give the proofs of this, unless I quote the whole of his writings!

Greater than all these, Jesus Christ himself had a remarkably tender and affectionate heart, and he expressed his righteousness very much in holy emotions. He had the greatest ardour, vigour and strength of love for God and men that ever existed. It was this holy love that triumphed in Gethsemane, when he wrestled with fear and grief, and when his soul was 'exceedingly sorrowful, even to death' (Matthew 26:38).

We see that Jesus had a strong and deep emotional life during his days on earth. We read of his great zeal for God: 'Zeal for your house has eaten me up' (John 2:17). We read of his grief for the sins of men: 'being grieved by the hardness of their hearts' (Mark 3:5). He even broke into tears when he considered the sin and misery of the ungodly people of Jerusalem: 'Now as he drew near, he saw the city and wept over it, saying, "If you had known, even you, especially in this your day, the things that make for your peace!"' (Luke 19:41-2). We often read of Jesus' pity and compassion; see Matthew 9:36, 14:14, 15:32, 18:34; Mark 6:34; Luke 7:13. How tender his heart was when Lazarus died! How affectionate were his parting words to his disciples the evening before he was crucified! Of all the speeches that ever came from the lips of men, the words of Christ in chapters 13 to 16 of John's Gospel are the most affectionate and the most affecting.

7.
Emotions in heaven.

Doubtless there is true religion in heaven. Heaven's religion, indeed, is absolutely pure and perfect. According to the pictures of heaven Scripture gives us, its religion consists mainly in love and joy, expressed in the most fervent and exalted praises. Now, the religion of the saints in heaven is the religion of earthly saints made perfect. Grace here is the dawn of glory hereafter. Texts such as 1 Corinthians 13 prove this. So if the religion of heaven is a religion of emotion, all true religion must be a religion of emotion.

The way to learn the true nature of anything is to go where that thing is found in its purity. We must therefore raise our minds to heaven, if we would know what true religion is. This is because all who are truly spiritual are not of this world. They are strangers here, and belong to heaven. They are born from above, and heaven is their native country. The nature which they receive from their heavenly birth is a heavenly nature. The life of true religion in the believer's heart is a seed of the religion of heaven, and God prepares us for heaven by conforming us to it. So if heaven's religion is one of emotion, ours on earth must be too.

8.
Emotions and our religious duties.

We see the importance of spiritual emotions from the duties God has appointed as expressions of worship.

Prayer. In prayer we declare God's perfections, his majesty, holiness, goodness and all-sufficiency, and our own emptiness and unworthiness, our needs and desires. But why? Not to inform God of these things, for he knows them anyway, and certainly not to change his purposes and persuade him that he ought to bless us. No, but we declare these things to move and affect our own hearts with what we express, and in this way to prepare ourselves to receive the blessings we ask.

Praise. The duty of singing praises to God seems to have no other purpose than to excite and express spiritual emotions. Only one reason can be given why God should command us to express ourselves to him in poetry as well as prose, and in song as well as speech. The reason is this: when divine truth is expressed in poetry and song, it has more of a tendency to impress itself on us and move our emotions.

Baptism and the Lord's supper. The same is true of baptism and the Lord's supper. Physical and visible things greatly influence us by nature. Therefore God has not only ordained that we should hear the gospel from his Word. He has also ordained that we should **see** the gospel displayed before our eyes in visible symbols, so that it will affect us more. These visible displays of the gospel are baptism and the Lord's supper.

Preaching. One great reason why God has appointed preaching in the Church is to impress divine truths on our hearts and emotions. It is not enough that we should have good commentaries and books of theology. These may enlighten our understandings, but they do not have the same power as preaching to move our wills. God uses the energy of the spoken word to apply his truth to our hearts in a more particular and lively way.

9. Emotions and hardness of heart.

Another proof that true religion lies very much in emotions is that Scripture often calls sin 'hardness of heart'. Consider these texts:

'So when he had looked around at them with anger, being grieved by the hardness of their hearts,' etc. (Mark 3:5).

'Today, if you will hear his voice: "Do not harden your hearts, as in the rebellion, and as in the day of trial in the wilderness, when your fathers tested me; they proved me, though they saw my work. For forty years I was grieved with that generation, and said, 'It is a people who go astray in their hearts'"' (Psalm 95:7-10).

'O Lord, why have you made us stray from your ways, and hardened our heart from your fear?' (Isaiah 63:17).

'But he stiffened his neck and hardened his heart against turning to the Lord God of Israel' (2 Chronicles 36:13).

Along with such texts, consider also that Scripture describes conversion as 'taking away the stony heart and giving a heart of flesh' (Ezekiel 11:19, 36:26).

A hard heart is obviously a heart which it is not easy to move or impress with spiritual emotions. It is like a stone — cold, insensitive, unfeeling towards God and holiness. It is the opposite of a heart of flesh, which has feeling and can be touched and moved. It follows, then, that holiness of heart consists mainly in spiritual emotions.

10.
What lessons about emotion can we learn from all this?

(i) We learn from this how great an error it is to reject all spiritual emotions as having nothing solid in them. This error can arise after a religious revival. Because the lively emotions of many seem so soon to vanish completely, people begin to despise all spiritual emotions, as if Christianity had nothing to do with them.

The other extreme is to look upon all lively religious emotions as signs of true conversion, without inquiring into the nature and source of those emotions. If people simply appear to be very warm and are full of spiritual talk, others conclude that they must be godly Christians.

Satan tries to push us from one extreme to the other. When he sees that emotions are in fashion, he sows his tares among the wheat. He mingles false emotions with the work of God's Spirit. In this way he deludes and eternally ruins many, confuses true believers, and corrupts Christianity. However, when the evil consequences of these false emotions become apparent, Satan changes his strategy. Now he tries to persuade people that all spiritual emotions are worthless. In this way he seeks to shut out everything spiritual from our hearts, and to turn Christianity into a lifeless formality.

The right way is neither to reject all emotions, nor to approve all, but to distinguish between them. We should approve some, and reject others. We must separate between the wheat and the chaff, the gold and the dross, the precious and the worthless.

(ii) If true religion lies much in our emotions, we should set a high value on what produces those emotions in us. We should desire the sort of books, and preaching, and praying, and singing, that will deeply affect our hearts.

Do not misunderstand me. These things can sometimes stir up the emotions of weak and ignorant people without doing any good to their souls. This is because it is possible for these things to excite emotions which are **not spiritual and holy emotions**. There has got to be a clear presentation and a right understanding of spiritual truth in our religious books, our preaching, our prayers and our songs. As long as this is the case, the more they move our emotions, the better they are.

(iii) If true religion lies much in our emotions, we have great cause for shame that spiritual realities do not affect us more.

God has given us emotions for the same purpose as all our other powers — to serve man's chief end, his relationship with God. Yet how common it is for human emotions to be taken up with anything except spiritual realities! In matters of people's worldly interests, their outward delights, their reputation, and their natural relations — in these things, their desires are eager, their love is warm, and their zeal is ardent.

Yet how insensitive and unmoved most people are about spiritual things! Here their love is cold, their desires are sluggish, and their gratitude is small. They can sit and hear about the infinite love of God in Jesus Christ, Christ's agonising death for sinners, and salvation by his blood from the everlasting fires of hell to the inexpressible joys of heaven — and be cold, unresponsive and uninterested! Yet what else should move our emotions, if not these truths? Could anything possibly be more important, more wonderful, or more relevant? Can any Christian entertain the thought that the glorious gospel of Jesus Christ should not stir and excite human emotions?

God planned our redemption so that it would reveal all the greatest truths in the most vivid and affecting way. The human personality and the human life of Jesus reveal the glory and beauty of God in the most moving way imaginable. Just as the cross shows Jesus' love for sinners in the most touching way, so it also reveals the hateful nature of our sins in the most affecting manner. For we see the dreadful effect which our sins had on Jesus, as he suffered for us. In the cross, too, we see the most impressive revelation of God's hatred of sin, and his justice and wrath in punishing it. Even though it was his own infinitely lovely Son who stood in the place of our sin, God struck him down to death. How strict must God's justice be, then, and how awful his holy anger!

And how great ought our shame to be, that these things do not affect us more!

Part Two.
Things which do NOT prove that our emotions come from a true experience of salvation.

Religious emotions can be natural or spiritual in origin. They can exist in people who are not saved, as well as in those who are truly converted. In this part of the book, I am going to examine experiences which prove **neither** that our emotions are spiritual **nor** that they are unspiritual in nature. In other words, I want us to look at experiences which tell us nothing about whether our emotions are spiritual or unspiritual.

1.
It does not prove that our emotions are spiritual, or unspiritual, if they are strong and lively.

Some people condemn all strong emotions. They feel prejudiced against anyone with powerful, lively feelings about God and spiritual things. They instantly assume that such people are deluded. Yet if, as I proved, true religion lies very much in our emotions, it follows that a great amount of true religion in a person's life will produce great emotions.

Love is an emotion, but will any Christian say that we should not love God or Jesus Christ in a large measure? Or will anyone say that we should not feel a great hatred and sorrow for sin? Or that we should not feel a high degree of gratitude to God for his mercy? Or that we should not have great desires after God and holiness? Is there any Christian who can say, 'I am quite satisfied with the amount of love and gratitude I feel towards God, and the amount of hatred and sorrow I feel towards sin. There is no need for me to pray for a deeper experience of these things'?

1 Peter 1:8 speaks of strong and lively emotions when it says 'you greatly rejoice with joy inexpressible and full of glory.' Indeed, Scripture often requires us to feel strongly. In the first and greatest commandment, Scripture strains language to express the degree in which we should love God: 'You shall love the Lord your God with all your heart, with all your soul, with all your mind, and with all your strength' (Mark 12:30). Scripture also commands us to feel high degrees of joy: 'Let

the righteous be glad; let them rejoice before God; yes, let them rejoice exceedingly' (Psalm 68:3). It also frequently calls on us to feel high degrees of gratitude for God's mercies.

The most outstanding believers whose experiences Scripture records often express lively emotions. As an example, let us take the psalmist. He mentions his love as if it were unspeakable: 'Oh, how I love your law!' (Psalm 119:97). He describes great degrees of spiritual desire: 'As the deer pants for the water brooks, so pants my soul for you, O God' (Psalm 42:1). He speaks of great grief for his own sins and the sins of others: 'My iniquities have gone over my head; like a heavy burden they are too heavy for me' (Psalm 38:4). 'Rivers of water run down from my eyes, because men do not keep your law' (Psalm 119:136). And he expresses fervent spiritual joy and praise: 'Because your loving-kindness is better than life, my lips shall praise you. Thus I will bless you while I live; I will lift up my hands in your name ... In the shadow of your wings I will rejoice' (Psalm 63:3-4, 7).

This proves that the existence of religious emotions in a very high degree is not necessarily a sign of fanaticism. We are in serious error if we condemn people as fanatics just because their emotions are strong and lively.

On the other hand, the fact that our emotions are strong and lively does not prove that they are truly spiritual in nature. Scripture shows us that people can become very excited about religion without being truly saved. In the Old Testament, for example, God's mercy to the Israelites at the exodus greatly stirred their emotions, and they sang his praises, Exodus 15:1-21. Yet they soon forgot his works. The giving of the law at Sinai stirred them up again; they seemed full of holy enthusiasm, and cried out, 'All that the Lord has spoken we will do!' (Exodus 19:8). Yet soon afterwards they were worshipping the golden calf!

In the New Testament, the crowds in Jerusalem professed great admiration for Christ, and praised him highly. 'Hosanna to the Son of David! Blessed is he who comes in the name of the Lord! Hosanna in the highest!' (Matthew 21:9). Yet how few of these were true disciples of Christ. Soon the same crowds would be crying out, 'Crucify him! Crucify him!' (Mark 15:13-14).

All orthodox theologians agree that feelings about Christianity can be very lively without any genuine experience of salvation.

2.
It does not prove that our emotions are spiritual, or unspiritual, if they produce great effects on the body.

All our emotions have an effect on our bodies. This is because of the intimate union between body and soul, flesh and spirit. It is not surprising, then, that strong emotions have a great effect on the body. However, strong emotions can be either natural or spiritual in origin. The presence of bodily effects cannot prove whether the experience is simply natural or truly spiritual.

Spiritual emotions, when powerful and deep, can certainly produce great bodily effects. The psalmist says, 'My heart and my flesh cry out for the living God' (Psalm 84:2). Here is a plain distinction between heart and flesh. His spiritual experience affected both. Again he says, 'My soul thirsts for you, my flesh longs for you' (Psalm 63:1). Here also there is a clear distinction between soul and flesh.

The prophet Habakkuk speaks of his sense of God's majesty overwhelming his body: 'When I heard, my body trembled, my lips quivered at the voice. Rottenness entered my bones; and I trembled in myself' (Habakkuk 3:16). We find the same in the psalmist, 'My flesh trembles for fear of you' (Psalm 119:120).

Scripture gives us accounts of revelations of God's glory which had powerful bodily effects on those who saw them. For instance, Daniel: 'No strength remained in me; for my vigour was turned to frailty in me, and I retained no strength' (Daniel 10:8). This is how the apostle John reacted to a vision of Christ: 'And when I saw him, I fell at his feet as one dead' (Revelation 1:17). It is no good objecting that these were outward and visible rather than spiritual revelations of God's glory. The outward glory was a **sign** of God's spiritual glory. Daniel and John would have understood this. The outward glory did not overwhelm them merely by its physical splendour, but precisely because it was a sign of the infinite spiritual glory of God. It would be presumptuous to say that in our day God never gives believers spiritual sights of his beauty and majesty which produce similar bodily effects.

On the other hand, bodily effects do not prove that the emotions which produce those effects are spiritual. Strong emotions which are not truly spiritual in origin can produce great bodily effects. Therefore we cannot point to mere bodily effects as a proof that our experience is from God. We must have some other way of testing the nature of our emotions.

[Note: Edwards spends almost the whole of this chapter arguing that spiritual emotions can produce great bodily effects (not that they always or even normally do so). We must remember that he was writing in the context of one of the greatest revivals known in Church history, when people were liable to swoon, weep and tremble under the powerful preaching of God's Word. Edwards was concerned to defend the integrity of the revival against the charge that such bodily phenomena proved it was all mere hysteria. Perhaps in our day — which at the moment of writing is not a day of revival —

Edwards might have altered his emphasis somewhat, and stressed that physical liveliness in worship is no guarantee whatever that the worship is genuine or that the Holy Spirit is present! — N.R.N.]

3. It does not prove that our emotions are spiritual, or unspiritual, if they produce a great warmth and readiness to talk about Christianity.

Many people have strong prejudices against those who speak warmly and readily about spiritual things. They condemn them as boastful hypocrites. On the other hand, many ignorantly assume that such ready talkers must be true children of God. 'God,' they say, 'has opened his mouth! He used to be slow to speak, but now he is full and free. He opens his heart, tells of his experiences, and praises God.' If this abundance of religious talk seems warm and serious, this especially convinces many people that it must be a sign of conversion.

However, it is not necessarily a sign of conversion. Those who think so are trusting their own ideas instead of submitting to holy Scripture as their guide. Scripture nowhere says that spiritual talk is a sure sign of conversion. Such talk may be just the religion of the tongue, which Scripture symbolises by the leaves of a tree. No tree should be without leaves, but leaves do not prove that the tree is a good tree.

Readiness to talk about spiritual things may be from a good cause, or it may be from a bad one. It may be because a person's heart is full of holy emotions — 'For out of the abundance of the heart the mouth speaks' (Matthew 12:34). On the other hand, it may be because his heart is full of emotions which are not holy. It is the nature of all strong emotions to prompt people to talk about the things that have affected them. Such talk will indeed be both earnest and warm. So then, people who talk freely and warmly about spiritual things are obviously excited about Christianity, but I have already shown that religious excitement can exist without a true experience of salvation.

Some people are over-full of talk about their experiences. They talk about them everywhere and in all company. This is a bad sign. A tree that is over-full of leaves does not usually bear much fruit. False emotions, if strong, are quicker to declare themselves than true emotions. It is the nature of false religion to love displaying itself, like the Pharisees.

4. It does not prove that our emotions are spiritual, or unspiritual, if we did not produce them by our own efforts.

Many condemn all emotions which do not arise from the natural workings of the mind. They ridicule the idea that we can actually feel the Holy Spirit working powerfully within us. The Spirit, they say, always works in a silent, unseen way. They insist that he only works through the truths of the Bible and through our own efforts, e.g. prayer. Therefore, they conclude, we have no way of distinguishing between the Spirit's work and the natural workings of our own minds.

It is true that we have no right to expect God's Spirit to work within us if we neglect such things as Bible-study and prayer.

It is also true that the Spirit works in many different ways. Sometimes he does work silently and unseen.

Even so, if the experience of salvation comes to us from God, why should we not **feel** that it does? We do not produce salvation by our own efforts. The natural workings of our minds do not produce salvation. Bible-study and prayer cannot by themselves produce salvation. It is the Spirit of the Almighty who produces salvation in our hearts. Why, then, should we not feel that it is the Spirit working within us? If we feel this, we only feel what is true.

We are wrong, then, to call people deluded just because they claim they have felt the Holy Spirit working within them. To call this a delusion would be like saying, 'You feel that your experience is from God. Well, this proves that your experience is not from God!'

Scripture describes the salvation of a sinner as a rebirth (John 3:3), a resurrection from the dead (Ephesians 2:5), a new creation (2 Corinthians 5:17). These descriptions have one thing in common. **They all describe events which the person experiencing them could not have produced**. God alone is the author of a sinner's regeneration, spiritual resurrection and new creation. Surely a sinner who experiences God working in his life in this way will realise that it is **God** who is saving him? Doubtless this is why Scripture describes salvation as regeneration, resurrection and new creation. These words all witness to the fact that our experience of salvation does not have its origin in ourselves.

In salvation, God works with a power which is obviously more than human. In this way he prevents us from boasting about what **we** have done. For example, when God saved his people in the Old Testament, their experience made it clear that they had not saved themselves. When God saved them from Egypt at the exodus, he first allowed them to feel their own helplessness. Then he redeemed them by his miraculous power. It was clear to them that God was their Saviour.

We see the same experience of God's power in most of the conversions which the New Testament describes. The Holy Spirit did not convert people in a silent, secret, gradual way. He usually converted them with a glorious display of supernatural power. Today people often regard such experiences of conversion as a sure sign of delusion!

On the other hand, we must not think that our emotions are truly spiritual just because we did not produce them by our own efforts. Some people try to prove that their emotions are from the Holy Spirit by this argument: 'I did not produce this experience myself. The experience came to me when I was not seeking it. I cannot make it come back again by my own efforts.'

This argument is unsound. An experience which does not come from ourselves might have come from a false spirit. There are many false spirits who disguise themselves as angels of light (2 Corinthians 11:14). They imitate the Spirit of God with great skill and power. Satan can work within us, and we can distinguish Satan's work from the natural workings of our own minds. For example, Satan fills the minds of some people with terrible blasphemies and vile suggestions. Those people are sure that these Satanic blasphemies and suggestions do not come from their own minds. I think it is just as easy for Satan's power to fill us with deceitful comforts and joys. We would certainly feel that these comforts and joys did not come from ourselves. However, that would not prove they had come from God! The trances and raptures of some religious fanatics are not from God, but from Satan.

We can also have experiences which come from God's Spirit but which do not save us, or do not prove that we are saved. We read in Hebrews 6:4-5 of people 'who were once enlightened, and have tasted the heavenly gift, and have become partakers of the Holy Spirit, and have tasted the good word of God and the powers of the age to come,' but who turn out to be unsaved (verses 6-8).

Religious experiences can also happen without the influence of a good or evil spirit. People who are impressionable and have lively imaginations can have strange emotions and impressions which they do not produce by their own efforts. We do not produce dreams by our own efforts when we are asleep. Imaginative people can have religious feelings and impressions which are like dreams even though they are awake.

5. It does not prove that our emotions are spiritual, or unspiritual, if they come to us accompanied by a Bible verse.

True spiritual emotions can come to us accompanied by a Bible verse. Such emotions are spiritual if they arise out of a spiritual understanding of the truth which that verse teaches.

On the other hand, it is no proof that an emotion is spiritual just because it arises from a Bible verse which comes suddenly and powerfully into the mind. Some people think this sort of experience is a sign that they are saved. They especially think this, if the Bible verses produce emotions of hope or joy. They say: 'The verse came suddenly in to my mind. It was as if God were speaking directly to me. I was not thinking about the verse when it came. I did not even know at first that such a verse was in the Bible!' Perhaps they will add: 'One verse after another came into my mind. The verses were all so positive and encouraging. I wept with joy. I could no longer doubt that God loved me.'

In this way, people persuade themselves that their emotions and experiences are from God, and that they are truly saved. However, their assurance is unsound. The Bible does not tell us to test the reality of our faith in this way. The Bible does not say that we are saved if Bible verses come suddenly into our minds. The Bible does not say that we are saved if positive and encouraging verses enter our minds and make us weep. And the Bible alone is our infallible rule of religious belief and practice.

Many people think that an experience must be from God if it involves God's Word, the Bible. This does not follow. All we can argue is that an experience must be right if **the Bible tells us we should have that experience**. An experience is not right just because it involved the Bible.

How do we know it is not Satan who is putting these Bible verses into our minds? Satan used the Bible to try to tempt and deceive Jesus himself (Matthew 4:6). If God allowed Satan to tempt Jesus through Bible verses, why should Satan not put Bible verses into **our** minds to deceive **us**? Why should he not even use positive and encouraging verses to delude us? The devil loves to produce false hopes and joys in the unsaved. He wants to persuade them that they are Christians before they have truly repented. Why should he not misuse encouraging Bible verses to produce this false assurance? After all, false teachers pervert the Scriptures in this way and deceive people. And false teachers are Satan's servants. Satan can do what his servants do.

6.
It does not prove that our emotions are spiritual, or unspiritual, if there seems to be love in them.

Love is the essence of true religion. So if people who claim to be Christians seem to be loving, this is often taken as proof that their Christianity must be real. The argument is that love must come from God, because Satan cannot love.

Unfortunately, even love can be imitated. In fact, the more excellent anything is, the more imitations there will be. Nobody makes imitation rocks and pebbles. Yet there are all too many imitation diamonds and rubies. It is the same with Christian virtues. The skill of Satan and the deceitfulness of men's hearts try more than anything else to imitate Christian love and humility, since these qualities reveal the beauty of Christian character in a special way.

Scripture teaches that people can seem to have Christian love without being saved. Jesus speaks of those who claim to be Christians, but whose love will not continue to the end. 'And because lawlessness will abound, the love of many will grow cold. But he who endures to the end shall be saved' (Matthew 24:12-13). This shows that if we have a love which does not endure to the end, but grows cold, we will not be saved.

We may feel a love for God and Christ, then, without a true and lasting experience of salvation. This was the case with many Jews in Jesus' day, who praised Jesus so highly and followed him day and night without food, drink or sleep. They said to Jesus, 'I will follow you wherever you go' (Matthew 8:19), and 'Hosanna to the Son of David!' (Matthew 21:9). However, their love was shown to be false, because it grew cold and did not endure.

The apostle Paul thought that there were people in his day

who had a false love for Christ. In Ephesians 6:24, Paul says, 'Grace be with all those who love our Lord Jesus Christ in sincerity.' Paul desired blessing for those who loved Christ with a sincere love. He must have believed there were others who had a love for Christ which was not sincere.

Christian love for other Christians can also be imitated. We see this in the relationship between Paul and the Christians of Galatia. They were ready to tear out their eyes and give them to Paul (Galatians 4:15). What an extravagant love! And yet Paul expresses his fear that he had laboured over them in vain (Galatians 4:11). Obviously Paul felt that their love for him might not have been true Christian love after all.

7.
It does not prove that our emotions are spiritual, or unspiritual, if we experience many kinds of them.

Clearly, there are imitations of all kinds of spiritual emotions. We have just seen how people can imitate Christian love, but there are imitations of other spiritual emotions too. Here are some examples: King Saul had a false sorrow for sin (1 Samuel 15:24-5, 26:21). The Samaritans had a false fear of God (2 Kings 17:32-3). Naaman the Syrian had a false gratitude after the miraculous cure of his leprosy (2 Kings 5:15). In Jesus' parable of the sower, the stony ground represents people who had a false spiritual joy (Matthew 13:20). The apostle Paul before his conversion had a false zeal for God (Galatians 1:14, Philippians 3:6). After his conversion, Paul said that many unbelieving Jews had this false zeal (Romans 10:2). Many

Pharisees had a false hope of eternal life (Luke 18:9-14, John 5:39-40).

Unsaved people, then, can have all sorts of false emotions which resemble true spiritual emotions. And there is no reason why they should not have many of these emotions at the same time.

For instance, the crowds who accompanied Jesus into Jerusalem seem to have had many religious emotions all at once. They were full of **admiration** and **love** for Jesus. They showed great reverence for him, and laid their clothes on the ground for him to walk on. They expressed great **gratitude** to him for the good works he had done. They expressed strong **desires** for God's kingdom to come, and had great **hopes** that Jesus was about to establish it. They were full of **joy** and **zeal** in their praises of Jesus and their eagerness to accompany him. Yet how few of these people were Jesus' true disciples!

The existence of many false emotions at the same time in the same person is no mystery. When one strong emotion arises, it naturally produces other emotions. This is especially the case if the first emotion to appear is love. As I said before, love is the chief of the emotions, and (so to speak) the fountain of the other emotions.

Picture to yourself someone who for a long time has felt a fear of hell. Satan comes and deceived him into thinking that God has forgiven his sins. Let us suppose Satan deceives him through a vision of a man with a beautiful smiling face and open arms. The sinner believes this is a vision of Christ. Or perhaps Satan deludes him with a voice saying, 'Son, your sins are forgiven,' which the sinner thinks is the voice of God. So the sinner believes he is saved, even though he has no spiritual understanding of the gospel.

What a variety of emotions would come into this sinner's mind! He would be full of love for his imaginary Saviour whom he thinks has saved him from hell. He would be full of gratitude for his imaginary salvation. He would feel an overwhelming joy. His emotions would move him to talk to others about his experience. It would be easy for him to be humble before his imaginary God. He would deny himself and zealously promote his imaginary religion, while the warmth of his emotions lasted.

All these religious emotions can arise together in this way. And yet the person we have depicted experiencing these emotions is not a Christian! His emotions have come from the natural workings of his own mind, not the saving work of God's Spirit. Anyone who doubts whether this is possible has little understanding of human nature.

8. It does not prove that our emotions are spiritual, or unspiritual, if comforts and joys seem to follow in a certain order.

Many people reject the idea that spiritual emotions and experiences should happen in a certain order. They do not think conviction of sin, fear of God's judgment, and a sense of spiritual helplessness need to come before the experience of conversion. This, they say, is only a human theory. So they are sceptical when a person's religious experiences do happen in this order. They suspect that his emotions have come from the natural workings of his own mind, rather than from the Holy Spirit. They are particularly suspicious if his feelings — first of conviction, then of assurance — are very strong and lively.

However, it is surely reasonable to think that God gives sinners a sense of their need of salvation before he saves them.

We are intelligent beings, and God deals with us in an intelligent way. If sinners are under condemnation outside of Christ, is it not reasonable that God should make them aware of this? After all, God makes Christians aware of their salvation once he has saved them.

Scripture teaches that God does make people aware of their helplessness before he sets them free. For example, before God brought Israel out of Egypt, he made them feel their misery and cry to him (Exodus 2:23). And before he saved them at the Red Sea, he made them see how helpless they were. The Red Sea was in front of them, and the Egyptian army behind them! God showed them that they could do nothing to help themselves, and that he alone could rescue them (Exodus 14). When Jesus and his disciples were caught in the storm on the Sea of Galilee, waves covered the ship, and it seemed to be about to sink. The disciples cried out, 'Lord, save us!' Only then did Jesus calm the wind and the waves (Matthew 8:24-6). The apostle Paul and Timothy, before God rescued them from trouble, 'were burdened beyond measure, above strength, so that we despaired even of life. Yes, we had the sentence of death in ourselves, that we should not trust in ourselves but in God who raises the dead' (2 Corinthians 1:8-9).

Scripture describes Christians as those 'who have fled for refuge to lay hold of the hope set before us' (Hebrews 6:18). Fleeing suggests fear and a sense of danger. In fact, the very word 'gospel' — good news — naturally suggests the idea of rescue and salvation from fear and distress. The crowds in Jerusalem felt this distress when Peter preached to them on the day of Pentecost. 'They were cut to the heart, and said to Peter and the rest of the apostles, "Men and brethren, what shall we do?"' (Acts 2:37). The Philippian gaoler also felt this spiritual distress. 'He fell down trembling before Paul and Silas. And he brought them out and said, "Sirs, what must I do to be saved?"' (Acts 16:29-30).

We see, then, how reasonable and Scriptural it is to think that great and humbling convictions of sin and helplessness, and fear of God's judgment, should come before the experience of conversion.

On the other hand, it is no proof that assurance of salvation is right just because it follows the fear of hell. The fear of hell, and a conviction of sin in the conscience, are two different things. Conviction of sin in the conscience is an awareness of personal disobedience and evil in an individual's own heart and life. It is a knowledge of how infinitely serious our own sin is, because it offends an infinitely holy God. This conviction can **produce** the fear of hell, but it is not the **same** as the fear of hell.

In fact, the fear of hell can exist without a true conviction of sin in the conscience. Some people seem to see hell opening up to swallow them, full of flames and devils. Yet their consciences are not convicted! These vivid impressions of hell can come from Satan. He can terrify men with visions of damnation because he wants to convince them they can never be saved. Such visions can also come from a man's own imagination.

There is also such a thing as a false conviction of sin. This happens when people seem overwhelmed with a feeling of how sinful they are, but they have no understanding of the true nature of sin. They do not see sin in a spiritual way, as something that offends God's holiness. Their consciences are untouched, or touched only slightly. Perhaps they have no conviction at all about particular sins of which they are guilty. Or if they are troubled about particular sins, they are not troubled in a spiritual way.

Even if the Holy Spirit himself produces conviction of sin and fear of hell, this will not necessarily lead to salvation. Unsaved people can resist the Spirit. God does not always intend to conquer sinful resistance and bring the sinner to new birth.

There is also such a thing as a false humbling before God. For example, King Saul felt deeply troubled about his sin against David. He wept before David, and confessed: 'You are more righteous than I; for you have rewarded me with good, whereas I have rewarded you with evil' (1 Samuel 24:17). Yet this was after the Spirit of God had departed from Saul.

Proud King Saul humbled himself before David, even though he really hated David! In a similar way, sinners can humble themselves before God, even though they really hate him. They can cease to trust in their own righteousness in some ways, but carry on trusting it in other, more subtle ways. Their apparent submission to God hides a secret attempt to bargain with him.

However, what if we experience the fear of hell **at the same time** as a conviction of sin which humbles us before God? And what if this then leads to joy in the gospel? Does this not prove that our experiences are spiritually genuine?

No! The order of our experiences proves nothing. If Satan can imitate the spiritual experiences which lead to conversion, he can imitate the order of them too. We know that he can produce a false conviction of sin, a false fear of hell, and a false humbling before God. Why should he not produce them in that order? And why should he not then produce a false joy in the gospel, as we have seen that he can do?

Scripture alone is our infallible guide to religious belief and practice. It does not say that we are saved if we have had experiences in a certain order. God's Word promises salvation only to those who receive God's grace and bring forth its fruits. It never promises salvation to those who feel great conviction of sin and fear of hell, followed by great joy and assurance. What Scripture says ought to be enough for Christians. Our trust is in God's Word, not our own ideas.

Before closing this chapter, I think I should point out that people **can** become Christians without passing through a **clear** order of experiences at all. It is true that they need to feel a conviction of sin, of helplessness, and of God's justice in condemning sinners. Even so, there is no need for God's Spirit to produce these things as **distinct** and **separate** experiences, one after another. In fact, the conversion of a sinner is sometimes like a confused chaos, and other Christians do not know how to interpret it!

The Holy Spirit often works in a very mysterious way in bringing people to Christ. As Jesus said, 'The wind blows where it wishes, and you hear the sound of it, but cannot tell where it comes from and where it goes. So is everyone who is born of the Spirit' (John 3:8).

In fact, ideas about how the Holy Spirit ought to work affect the way we interpret our experience. We pick out the parts of our conversion which most resemble the experiences we think should happen in conversion. We forget other parts of our conversion which do not fit into what we consider the proper pattern. In this way, we try to force our conversion into conformity with a so-called 'right pattern' of experience. What we are really doing is refusing to admit that the Holy Spirit sometimes works differently to the precise way **we** want him to work!

9.
It does not prove that our emotions are spiritual, or unspiritual, if they cause us to spend much time in the outward duties of Christian worship.

Some people think a religious experience is unhealthy, if it causes us to spend much time in reading, praying, singing and hearing sermons. By contrast, Scripture clearly teaches that a true experience of salvation will have this effect.

For example, Anna the prophetess 'did not depart from the temple, but served God with fastings and prayers night and day' (Luke 2:37). Daniel had a time of private prayer three times every day (Daniel 6:10). The experience of salvation also causes believers to delight in singing praises to God: 'Praise the Lord! For it is good to sing praises to our God; for it is pleasant, and praise is beautiful' (Psalm 147:1). Salvation causes believers to love to hear God's Word preached: 'How beautiful on the mountains are the feet of him who brings good news, who proclaims peace, who brings glad tidings of good things, who proclaims salvation, who says to Zion, "Your God reigns!"' (Isaiah 52:7). And salvation makes believers love to worship with other believers: 'How lovely is your tabernacle, O Lord of hosts! My soul longs, yes, even faints for the courts of the Lord ... Blessed are those who dwell in your house; they will still be praising you' (Psalm 84:1-2,4).

On the other hand, it is no sure sign of conversion if we are enthusiastic in the outward duties of true religion. Such behaviour exists in many who are not saved. The Jews in Isaiah's time were enthusiastic in worship. They had many sacrifices, assemblies, festivals, and prayers. Yet their hearts were not right with God, and God tells them he hates their worship! (See Isaiah 1:12-15). In Ezekiel's time, many delighted in hearing Ezekiel preach God's Word. However, God condemns them: 'So they come to you as people do, they sit before you as my people, and they hear your words, but they do not do them; for with their mouth they show much love, but their hearts pursue their own gain. Indeed, you are to them as a very lovely song of one who has a pleasant voice and can play well on an instrument; for they hear your words, but they do not do them' (Ezekiel 33:31-2).

10.
It does not prove that our emotions are spiritual, or unspiritual, if they cause us to praise God with our mouths.

Many seem to think that if people are enthusiastic in praising God, this is a sure sign of conversion. I briefly looked at this in the previous chapter. I want to examine it in more detail here, because of the great emphasis some people put on praise as a sign of spiritual life.

No Christian will condemn another person for enthusiasm in praising God. Nevertheless, we must realise that such enthusiasm is not a sure sign of conversion. As we have already seen, Satan can imitate all kinds of spiritual emotions. And Scripture gives us many examples of unsaved people praising God and Christ enthusiastically.

When Jesus performed miracles at various times, Scripture says that the crowds 'all were amazed and glorified God' (Mark 2:12), 'they glorified the God of Israel' (Matthew 15:31), 'fear came upon them all, and they glorified God' (Luke 7:16). They were also enthusiastic in praising Jesus himself. 'And he taught in their synagogues, being glorified by all' (Luke 4:15). 'Hosanna to the son of David! Blessed is he who comes in the name of the Lord! Hosanna in the highest!' (Matthew 21:9) Sadly, we know how few of these people had a real saving faith in God and Christ.

After Jesus had ascended to heaven, we read in Acts that those who lived in Jerusalem 'all glorified God for what had been done' (Acts 4:21). This was because Peter and John had miraculously healed a lame beggar. Yet how few of those living in Jerusalem shared the faith of Peter and John! When Paul and Barnabas preached to the Gentiles in Antioch, the

Gentiles 'were glad and glorified the word of the Lord' (Acts 13:48). However, only some were saved; for 'as many as had been appointed to eternal life believed.'

Israel sang God's praises at the Red Sea, but they were soon worshipping the golden calf. The Jews in Ezekiel's time showed much love for God with their mouths, but their hearts were in love with money and possessions (Ezekiel 33:31-2). Isaiah says that those who hated God's true servants were crying out, 'Let the Lord be glorified' (Isaiah 66:5).

From these and many other Scripture examples, it follows that enthusiasm in praising God and Christ is not a reliable sign of conversion.

11.
It does not prove that our emotions are spiritual, or unspiritual, if they produce assurance of salvation.

Some people think that we must be deluded if we have assurance of our salvation. By contrast, Protestants have always believed that assurance is a proper feeling in a Christian. Scripture contains many examples of God's people feeling sure of their relationship with God.

For instance, David often speaks in the Psalms about God as his own God and Saviour, his rock and shield and tower, and so on. The apostle Paul in his letters constantly speaks of his relationship with Christ, and rejoices in his salvation. 'I know whom I have believed and am persuaded that he is able to keep what I have committed to him until that day' (2 Timothy 1:12).

It is clear from Scripture that all Christians — not just apostles and prophets — can and should have this assurance.

Peter commands us to make certain about God's calling and choice of us (2 Peter 1:10), and tells us how to obtain this certainty (2 Peter 1:5-8). Paul speaks about lack of assurance as something highly unsuitable in a Christian: 'Examine yourselves as to whether you are in the faith. Prove yourselves. Do you not know yourselves, that Jesus Christ is in you? — unless indeed you are disqualified' (2 Corinthians 13:5). John gives us many tests by which we can be sure we are saved: 'Now by this we know that we know Christ, if we keep his commandments' (1 John 2:3). 'We know that we have passed from death to life, because we love the brethren' (1 John 3:14). 'By this we know that we abide in him, and he in us, because he has given us of his Spirit (1 John 4:13).

It is very unreasonable, then, to criticise a Christian just because he feels a deep assurance of his own salvation.

On the other hand, it is no proof that a person is saved just because he feels sure that he is. A person may have the greatest and liveliest assurance of salvation, and yet still be unsaved. He may seem to be very close to God, and use very bold and affectionate language in his prayers, calling God 'my Father', 'my dear Redeemer', 'my sweet Saviour', 'my beloved', and so on. He may say, 'I know with complete certainty that God is my Father. I know that I will go to heaven, just as surely as if I were already there.' He may be so sure of himself that he no longer sees any reason to test the reality of his faith. He may despise anyone who suggests that he might not really be saved. However, none of this proves he is a true Christian.

In fact, this sort of boastful assurance, which is always making a display of itself, does not look like real Christian assurance at all. It seems more like the Pharisee in Luke 18:9-14, who was so sure he was right with God, and thanked God boldly for making him so different from other men! True Christian assurance is humble, not boastful.

The hearts of unsaved people are blind, deceitful and self-centred. It is not surprising that they have such high opinions of themselves. And if Satan works on their sinful desires with false comforts and joys, it is not surprising that unconverted people should have a strong but false assurance of salvation.

When an unsaved person has this false assurance, he is free from those things which can cause a real Christian to doubt his own salvation:

(i) The false Christian has no sense of the seriousness of his eternal destiny, and the infinite importance of building on a right foundation. By contrast, the true believer is humble and cautious; he feels what a great thing it will be to stand before God, the infinitely holy Judge. False assurance knows nothing of this.

(ii) A false Christian is not aware of how blind and deceitful his heart is. His false assurance produces a great confidence in his own opinions. The true believer, however, has a modest view of his own understanding.

(iii) Satan does not attack false assurance. He attacks the assurance of the true Christian, because true assurance produces greater holiness. On the other hand, Satan is the best friend of false assurance, because it places the false Christian completely in his power.

(iv) False assurance blinds a person to the true extent of his sinfulness. The false Christian seems clean and bright in his own eyes. The true Christian, by contrast, knows his own heart; he feels he is a great sinner. He often wonders whether a truly saved person could possibly be as sinful as he knows he himself is.

There are two kinds of false Christian. There are those who think they are Christians because of their mere external practice of morality and religion. These people often do not understand the doctrine of justification by faith alone. Then there are those whose assurance comes from false religious experiences.

It is this last kind of false Christians who are the worst. Their assurance often comes from supposed revelations. They call these revelations 'the witness of the Spirit'. They experience visions and impressions; they may claim that God's Spirit has revealed future events to them. It is no wonder that people who accept such experiences also have visions and impressions about their own salvation. And it is no wonder if a supposed revelation about their salvation produces the highest degree of assurance.

In fact, great confidence is a distinguishing mark of people who seek guidance from imaginary revelations. They boldly say, 'I know this or that,' 'I know for certain.' They despise all argument and rational inquiry which might make them doubt their experience.

It is easy to understand the confidence of these people. It pleases their self-love to think God has told them in a special way that they are his dear children. And it increases their false assurance if these 'revelations' come with vivid emotions, which they misinterpret as the Holy Spirit working within them.

Now I would give a word of warning to preachers: you sometimes preach true doctrines in a wrong way which encourages a false assurance! You tell people to 'live by faith, not by sight', to 'trust God in the dark', and to 'trust in Christ, not in our feelings'. These are true doctrines **if rightly understood.**

To live by faith, not by sight, means allowing invisible heavenly realities to control our thoughts and attitudes. We cannot see God or Christ with our physical eyes. We cannot **see** the new heavens and new earth, for they have not yet been established. Instead, we **believe** in these unseen realities. To believe in them, and to let this belief rule our hearts and lives — this is living by faith, not by sight.

By contrast, many think that 'living by faith, not by sight' means that we should trust in Christ, even though our hearts remain spiritually dark and dead. This is unscriptural and absurd. It is impossible to have faith in Christ and yet remain in spiritual darkness and death. True faith means coming out of spiritual darkness and death into Christ's light and life. To tell someone to trust in Christ although his heart remains dark and dead, is to tell him to have faith in Christ even though he remains an unbeliever!

Scripture teaches that faith in Christ involves a spiritual sight of him. Jesus said that 'everyone who sees the Son and believes in him' will have eternal life (John 6:40). True faith only exists when we are 'beholding as in a mirror the glory of the Lord', and seeing 'the light of the knowledge of the glory of God in the face of Jesus Christ' (2 Corinthians 3:18 and 4:6). A faith lacking this spiritual light is not the faith of the children of light, but the delusion of the children of darkness.

To 'trust God in the dark' means trusting his Word when our circumstances are dark and painful, as though God no longer cared for us. It also means continuing to trust him when we do not have such clear and refreshing views of his love as at other times. This is totally different from trusting God without any spiritual light or experience, with dead and worldly hearts!

Those who insist on living by faith without spiritual experience have absurd ideas of faith. What they really mean by 'faith' is believing that they are saved. That is why they think it is sinful to doubt their salvation, no matter how dead and worldly they are. Yet from what Bible have they discovered that faith means believing we are saved? The Bible says that faith **brings** sinners into salvation. So faith cannot mean believing we are **already** saved. If faith means believing we are saved, it would mean believing that we have saving faith. That is, faith would mean believing that we believe!

I admit that unbelief may be the cause of a lack of assurance. Some Christians have little faith; and little faith produces little evidence of salvation. The answer to this problem is to grow in faith, and produce more of the fruits of faith. Other Christians lack assurance despite many proofs in their lives that they are converted. Their doubt comes from a one-sided sense of their unworthiness, and a weak sense of the reality and power of God's mercy. Other Christians lack assurance because of their dark and painful circumstances. How can God love them if he lets them suffer so much? This doubt comes from a lack of dependence on God's sovereignty and wisdom.

Nevertheless, if someone feels that his heart is completely dead and worldly, we cannot blame him for doubting his salvation. It is impossible for true Christian assurance to exist in such a heart. It would be as impossible as trying to keep the sunshine after the sun had set. Memories of religious experiences we once had cannot keep assurance alive, if our hearts are now dark with sin.

In fact, it is **desirable** that we should doubt our salvation if our hearts feel totally dark and worldly. This is according to God's plan. When love for God decreases, anxiety for ourselves increases. In times of spiritual deadness, we need such anxiety to restrain us from sin, and to spur us to fresh spiritual effort.

We contradict God's plan, then, if we tell people to keep up their assurance when their hearts are worldly and dead. We are in serious error if we think this is what it means to 'live by faith, not by sight', to 'trust God in the dark', or to 'trust in Christ, not in our feelings'. To encourage assurance in those whose hearts are worldly and dead, is to encourage false assurance.

On the other hand, if we use our spiritual emotions and Christian experience as evidences of our salvation, this is not 'trusting in our feelings instead of in Christ'. There are no other evidences of salvation we can use! We are only 'trusting in our feelings instead of in Christ' if we praise and admire ourselves for our emotions. When our experiences and emotions become more important to us than God, and when we think that God himself should admire us for our wonderful emotions — then we are in danger. In fact, then we are in a worse spiritual condition than an immoral atheist!

12.
We cannot know that someone's emotions are spiritual, or unspiritual, just because he gives a moving account of them.

No Christian can infallibly distinguish between true and false believers. A Christian can see into his own heart, but he cannot see into anyone else's. All we can see in others is the outward appearance. And Scripture clearly teaches that we can never infallibly judge a person's heart from his outward appearance. 'The Lord does not see as man sees; for man looks at the outward appearance, but the Lord looks at the heart' (1 Samuel 16:7).

When a person seems outwardly, as far as we can tell, to be a Christian, it is our duty to accept him as a brother in Christ. Yet even the wisest Christian can be deceived. People who have seemed to be outstanding converts have often fallen away from faith.

This should not surprise us. We have already seen how Satan can imitate all kinds of spiritual emotions — love for God and Christ and Christians, sorrow for sin, submission to God, humility, gratitude, joy, zeal. All these imitated emotions can appear at the same time in the same person. And that person might also have a good knowledge of Christian doctrine, a likeable personality, and a powerful ability to express himself in Christian language.

How great the resemblance can be, then, between a false and a true Christian! Only God can infallibly tell the difference. We are arrogant if we pretend we can.

It does not prove that someone is a true Christian just because he gives a moving account of his feelings and experiences. Anything which resembles a work of God is bound to be moving to a believer. Believers love to see sinners converted. It is not surprising, then, that it touches our hearts when someone professes conversion and gives a plausible account of his experience. Still, that does not prove that his conversion is genuine.

Scripture tells us to judge by a person's life, not his talk. This is because the claims people make that they are Christians, are like blossoms in the spring. There are many blossoms on the trees, and they all look beautiful, but soon many of these blossoms will wither, drop off and rot. For a time, they look as beautiful as the other blossoms, and smell very sweet. We cannot distinguish the blossoms which will bear fruit from those which will wither and die. It is only afterwards that we can tell the difference, when some have fallen and others borne fruit.

It is the same in spiritual things. We must judge by the fruit, not by the beautiful colours and scent of the blossom. People who claim they have been converted may (so to speak) look beautiful, and smell sweet, and give moving accounts of their experience. However, it may all come to nothing. **Talk proves nothing**. We must judge by the fruit — by the lasting results in people's lives. (Even here, we cannot judge infallibly, but the way professing Christians live is the **best** proof we can have of their sincerity and salvation).

Some argue as follows: 'If I feel a strong Christian love for a fellow Christian, the Holy Spirit must have produced this love. But the Spirit cannot make mistakes. If the Spirit produces this love, he must know that the other person is a true Christian.'

This argument is completely false. God has commanded us to love as our fellow Christians **all who make a credible profession of faith in Christ**. So a strong Christian love for another professing Christian only proves that God's Spirit is enabling us to obey God's command. It does not prove that the professing Christian whom we love is a true Christian.

In any case, the Bible knows nothing of this idea that we can judge another person's spiritual condition by the love we feel for him. Not only is this idea absent from the Bible, it contradicts the Bible. God's Word clearly teaches that no-one can be one hundred per cent certain about the condition of another person's heart towards God. Paul says, 'he is a Jew who is one inwardly, and circumcision is that of the heart, in the Spirit, and not in the letter; whose praise is not from men but from God' (Romans 2:29). By this last expression, 'whose praise is not from men but from God,' Paul teaches that men cannot judge whether a man is a Jew 'inwardly'. Men can see by outward signs that a man is outwardly a Jew, but only God can see into a man's inward self.

Paul teaches the same truth in 1 Corinthians 4:5: 'judge nothing before the time, until the Lord comes, who will both bring to light the hidden things of darkness and reveal the counsels of the hearts; and then each one's praise will come from God.'

Surely we are being very arrogant if we think **we** can judge men's hearts, when the apostle did not think that **they** could!

Part Three.
The distinguishing signs of true spiritual emotions.

Opening remarks.

I am now going to point out some of the things which distinguish true spiritual emotions from other kinds of emotion. First, however, I want to lay down the following guidelines:

(i) I am not going to help anybody to distinguish infallibly between true and false spiritual emotions in **other people.** I have already condemned these attempts as arrogant. As far as judging others is concerned, Christ has only given us enough rules for our own safety, to prevent us from being led astray. He has also given us many rules in Scripture which church leaders will find useful in counselling church members about their spiritual state. However, God has not enabled us to make an infallible separation between the sheep and the goats among professing Christians. He had kept this power for himself alone.

(ii) I am not going to help Christians who have grown spiritually cold to obtain assurance of their salvation. I have already argued that it is not God's plan that such Christians should have assurance. God does not want them to be assured of their salvation except by coming out of their spiritually cold condition. We gain assurance, not so much by **self-examination**, as by **action**. The apostle Peter tells us to make our calling and election sure, not in the first place by self-examination, but by adding to our faith moral excellence, and knowledge, and self-control, and perseverance, and godliness, and brotherly kindness, and love (2 Peter 1:5-7). The spiritually cold Christian, then, should carry out Peter's instructions, instead of expecting help to know his salvation while he continues in a cold condition.

(iii) No-one should expect to find rules which will convict hypocrites deluded by imaginary revelations and false emotions, who have become fixed in a false assurance. Such hypocrites are so sure of their own wisdom, and so blinded by a subtle self-righteousness disguising itself as humility, that they often seem beyond repentance. However, these rules will be useful to convict other kinds of hypocrite, and also real Christians who have mixed false emotions with true.

1.
True spiritual emotions arise from spiritual, supernatural and divine influences on the heart.

The New Testament calls Christians **spiritual** people. It contrasts them with people who are merely **natural**. 'The natural man does not receive the things of the Spirit of God, for they are foolishness to him; nor can he know them, because they are spiritually discerned. But he who is spiritual judges all things' (1 Corinthians 2:14-15). It also makes a contrast between spiritual and **carnal** people. 'And I, brethren, could not speak to you as to spiritual people but as to carnal' — that is, to those who were in a large degree unsanctified (1 Corinthians 3:1). The terms 'natural' and 'carnal' in these verses mean unsanctified, lacking the Spirit. 'Spiritual', then, means sanctified by the Holy Spirit.

Just as Scripture calls Christians spiritual, we also find that it describes certain qualities and principles in the same way. We read of a 'spiritual mind' (Romans 8:6-7), 'spiritual understanding' (Colossians 1:9), and 'spiritual blessings' (Ephesians 1:3).

The term 'spiritual' in all these verses does not refer to the spirit of man. A quality is not spiritual just because it exists in man's spirit as opposed to his body. Scripture calls some qualities 'carnal' or 'fleshly', even though they exist in man's spirit. For example, Paul describes pride, self-righteousness and trusting in one's own wisdom as 'fleshly' (Colossians 2:18), although all these qualities exist in man's spirit.

The New Testament uses the term 'spiritual' to refer to the Holy Spirit, the Third Person of the Trinity. **Christians** are spiritual because they are born of God's Spirit and because the Spirit lives within them. **Things** are spiritual because of their relationship to the Holy Spirit — 'These things we also speak, not in words which man's wisdom teaches but which the Holy Spirit teaches, comparing spiritual things with spiritual. But the natural man does not receive the things of the Spirit of God' (1 Corinthians 2:13).

God gives his Spirit to true Christians to live within them, and to influence their hearts as a source of life and action. Paul says that Christians live by Christ living in them (Galatians 2:20). Christ by his Spirit not only **is** in them, but **lives** in them; they live by his life. Christians not only drink living water, but this living water becomes a fountain in their souls, springing up into spiritual and everlasting life (John 4:14). The sap of the true vine does not flow into them as into a cup, but into living branches, where the sap becomes a source of life (John 15:5). Scripture, then, calls Christians 'spiritual', because God unites his Spirit to them in this way.

The Spirit of God can and does influence natural men; see Numbers 24:2, 1 Samuel 10:10, Hebrews 6:4-6. In these cases, however, God does not give his Spirit as a source of spiritual life. There is no union between the Spirit of God and the natural man. I can illustrate this in the following way. Light may shine on a very dark, black object; but if the light does not cause the object itself to give off light, no-one would call it a bright object. So when the Spirit of God only acts **upon** the soul, but does not become a source of spiritual life **within** it, that soul has not become spiritual.

The main reason why Scripture calls Christians and their virtues 'spiritual' is this: the Holy Spirit within Christians produces results which are in harmony with the Spirit's own true nature.

Holiness is the nature of the Spirit of God; therefore Scripture calls him the **Holy** Spirit. Holiness is the beauty and sweetness of the divine nature, and is the essence of the Holy Spirit, just as heat is the nature of fire. This Holy Spirit lives in the hearts of Christians as a fountain of life, acting within them and giving himself to them in his sweet and divine nature of holiness. He causes the soul to share in God's spiritual beauty and Christ's joy, so that the believer has fellowship **with** the Father and **with** the Son, by participating **in** the Holy Spirit. So the spiritual life in the hearts of believers is the same in nature as God's own holiness, though infinitely less in degree. It is like the sun shining on a diamond. The diamond's brightness is the same in nature as the sun's brightness, but less in degree. This is what Christ means in John 3:6, 'that which is born of the Spirit is spirit.' The new nature which the Holy Spirit creates is the same in nature as the Spirit who created it; so Scripture calls it a spiritual nature.

It is only in true Christians that the Spirit works in this way. Jude describes worldly-minded men 'not having the Spirit' (Jude 19). Paul says that only true Christians have the Holy Spirit within them; and 'if anyone does not have the Spirit of Christ, he is not Christ's' (Romans 8:9). Having the Holy Spirit is a sure sign of being in Christ, according to John: 'By this we know that we abide in him, and he in us, because he has given us of his Spirit' (1 John 4:13). By contrast, a natural man has no experience of spiritual things; to talk about such things is foolishness to him, for he does not know what it means. 'The natural man does not receive the things of the Spirit of God, for they are foolishness to him; nor can he know them, because they are spiritually discerned' (1 Corinthians 2:14). Jesus himself taught that the unbelieving world has no acquaintance with the Holy Spirit: 'the Spirit of truth, whom the world cannot receive, because it neither sees him nor knows him' (John 14:17).

This much is clear, then: the effects which the Holy Spirit produces in true Christians are different from anything men can produce by natural human powers. This is what I meant when I said that true spiritual emotions arise from **supernatural** influences.

From this it follows that Christians have a new inward perception or sensation in their minds, entirely different in its nature from anything they experienced before they were converted. It is, so to speak, a new spiritual sense for spiritual things. This sense is different from any natural sense, just as the sense of taste is different from the senses of sight, hearing, smell and touch. By this new spiritual sense, the Christian perceives something different from anything the natural man perceives; it is like the difference between merely looking at honey and actually tasting its sweetness. This is why Scripture often compares the Spirit's work of regeneration to the giving of a new sense — sight to the blind, hearing to the deaf. And because this spiritual sense is more noble and excellent than any other, Scripture compares its bestowal to raising the dead and a new creation.

Many people confuse this new spiritual sense with the imagination, but it is quite different from the imagination. Imagination is an ability common to everyone. It enables us to have ideas of sights, sounds, odours and other things, even when those things are not present. Yet people do confuse imagination with the spiritual sense, in the following way. Some people have ideas impressed on their imagination of a bright light; they call this a spiritual revelation of God's glory. Some have lively ideas of Christ hanging and bleeding on the cross; they call this a spiritual sight of Christ crucified. Some see Christ smiling at them, with his arms open to embrace them; they call this a revelation of Christ's grace and love. Some have vivid ideas of heaven, and of Christ on his throne there, and shining ranks of angels and saints; they call this seeing heaven opened to them. Some have ideas of sounds and voices, perhaps quoting Scripture to them; they call this hearing the voice of Christ in their hearts, or having the witness of the Holy Spirit.

Yet these experiences have nothing spiritual or divine about them. They are simply imaginary ideas of external things — a light, a man, a cross, a throne, a voice. These imaginary ideas are not spiritual in nature. A natural man can have vivid ideas of shapes and colours and sounds. The imaginary idea of an external brightness and glory of God is no better than the idea millions of damned unbelievers will receive on Judgment Day of the external glory of Christ. A mental image of Christ hanging on a cross is no better than what the unspiritual Jews had, who stood round the cross and saw Christ with their physical eyes. Think about it. Is a picture of Christ in a person's imagination any better than the idea of Christ which Roman Catholics get from their idolatrous paintings and statues of him? And are the emotions which these imaginary ideas inspire any better than what ignorant Catholics feel when they worship these paintings and statues?

These imaginary ideas are so far from being spiritual in nature, that Satan can very easily produce them. If he can suggest **thoughts** to men, he can also suggest **images**. We know from the Old Testament that false prophets had dreams and visions from false spirits; see Deuteronomy 13:1-3, 1 Kings 22:21-3, Isaiah 28:7, Ezekiel 13:1-9, Zechariah 13:2-4. And if Satan can impress the mind with these imaginary ideas, they cannot be evidence that it is God at work.

Even if God did produce these ideas in someone's mind, it would prove nothing about that person's salvation. This is clear from the Scripture example of Balaam. God impressed a clear and vivid image on Balaam's mind of Jesus Christ as the star rising out of Jacob and the sceptre rising from Israel. Balaam described this experience as follows: 'The utterance of him who hears the words of God, and knows the knowledge of the Most High, who sees the vision of the Almighty, who falls down, with eyes opened wide. I see him, but not now; I behold him, but not near; a star shall come out of Jacob, and a sceptre shall rise out of Israel' (Numbers 24:16). Balaam saw Christ in a vision, but he had no spiritual knowledge of Christ. He was unsaved, despite this God-given image in his mind of the Saviour.

Emotions arising out of ideas in the imagination are not spiritual. Spiritual emotions can produce these ideas, especially in weak-minded people, but ideas in the imagination cannot produce spiritual emotions. Spiritual emotions can only arise from spiritual causes — from the Holy Spirit giving us spiritual understanding of spiritual truth. However, the mental idea of a sight or a voice is not spiritual in nature. It is something believers and unbelievers alike can experience, since imagination is a natural ability shared by everyone. Still, it is not surprising that imaginary religious ideas often stir up **natural** emotions to a high degree. What else should we expect, when the person who has these ideas believes they are divine revelations and signs of God's favour? Of course he becomes excited!

This may be a good place to say something about the witness of the Holy Spirit with our spirit that we are God's children (Romans 8:16). I find there are many who misunderstand this. They think the Spirit's witness is an immediate revelation of the fact that they are God's adopted children. It is as though God inwardly spoke to them, by a kind of secret voice or impression, assuring them that he is their Father.

It is the word 'witness' that misleads these people into thinking this. When Scripture says that God 'bears witness', they assume it must mean that God directly asserts or reveals truth. A more careful look at Scripture shows this to be incorrect. By 'bearing witness' or 'testifying', the New Testament often means **presenting evidence from which a thing may be proved true**. For example, in Hebrews 2:4 we read of 'God also bearing witness both with signs and wonders, with various miracles, and gifts of the Holy Spirit.' These signs, wonders, miracles and gifts are called God's witness, not because they were assertions, but because they were evidences and proofs. Again, we have 1 John 5:8, where John calls 'the water and the blood' witnesses. The water and blood did not assert anything, but they were evidence. Again, God's works of providence in rain and fruitful seasons are 'witnesses' to God's goodness — that is, they are evidences of these things (Acts 14:17).

When Paul speaks of the Holy Spirit witnessing with our spirit that we are God's children, he does not mean that the Spirit makes some supernatural suggestion or revelation to us. The previous verses show what Paul means: 'For as many as are led by the Spirit of God, these are sons of God. For you did not receive a spirit of bondage again to fear, but you received the spirit of adoption by whom we cry out, "Abba, Father." The Spirit himself bears witness with our spirit that we are children of God' (Romans 8:14-16). This means that the Holy Spirit gives us **evidence** that we are God's children, by dwelling in us, leading us, and inclining us to behave towards God as children of a father.

Paul speaks of two spirits, the spirit of slavery, which is fear, and the spirit of adoption, which is love. The spirit of slavery works by fear. The slave fears punishment, but loves cries, 'Abba! Father!' and enables a man to go to God and behave as his child. In this childlike love for God, the believer sees and feels the union of his soul with God. From this he is assured that he is God's child. So the witness of the Holy Spirit is not some spiritual whisper or immediate revelation. It is the holy effect of God's Spirit in the hearts of believers, leading them to love

God, hate sin and pursue holiness. Or, as Paul puts it: 'If you live according to the flesh, you will die; but if by the Spirit you put to death the deeds of the body, you will live' (Romans 8:13).

When Paul says that the Holy Spirit bears witness with **our** spirit, he does not mean there are two separate independent witnesses. He means that we receive by our spirit the witness of God's Spirit. That is, our spirit sees and declares the evidence of our adoption which the Holy Spirit produces in us. Our spirit is the part of us Scripture elsewhere calls the heart (1 John 3:19-21) and the conscience (2 Corinthians 1:12).

Terrible harm has resulted from thinking that the Holy Spirit's witness is a kind of inward voice, suggestion or declaration from God to a man, that he is loved, forgiven, elect and so forth. How many lively but false emotions have arisen from this delusion! I fear that multitudes have gone to hell deceived by it. That is why I have dealt with it at such length.

2.
The object of spiritual emotion is the loveliness of spiritual things, not our self-interest.

I do not mean to exclude all self-interest from spiritual emotions, but its place is secondary. The primary object of spiritual emotions is the excellence and beauty of spiritual things as they are in themselves, not the relation they have to our self-interest.

Some people say that all love arises out of self-love. It is impossible, they say, for anyone to love God without self-love being at the root of it. According to them, whoever loves God and desires fellowship with God and the glory of God, only desires these things for the sake of his own happiness. So a desire for one's own happiness (self-love) lies at the root of love for God. However, those who say this ought to ask themselves **why** a person places his happiness in fellowship with God and the glory of God. Surely this is the effect of love for God. A person must love God before he will regard fellowship with God and God's glory as his own happiness.

Of course, there is a kind of love for another person which arises out of self-love. This happens when the first thing that attracts our love to a person is some favour he shows us or some gift he gives us. In this case, self-love certainly lies at the root of love for another. It is completely different when the first thing that attracts our love to another is our appreciation of qualities in him which are lovely and beautiful in themselves.

Love for God which arises essentially out of self-love cannot be spiritual in nature. Self-love is a purely natural principle. It exists in the hearts of devils as well as angels. So nothing can be spiritual if it is merely the result of self-love. Christ speaks about this in Luke 6:32: 'If you love those who love you, what credit is that to you? For even sinners love those who love them.'

The deepest cause of true love for God is **the supreme loveliness of God's nature**. This is the only reasonable thing to believe. What chiefly makes a man or any creature lovely is his excellence. Surely the same is true of God. God's nature is infinitely excellent; it is infinite beauty, brightness, and glory itself. How can we rightly love God's excellence and beauty, if we do not love them for their own sakes? People whose love for God is based on God's usefulness to them, are beginning at the wrong end. They are regarding God only from the viewpoint of their own self-interest. They are failing to appreciate the infinite glory of God's nature, which is the source of all goodness and all loveliness.

Natural self-love can produce many emotions towards God and Christ, where there is no appreciation of the beauty and glory of the divine nature. For instance, self-love can produce a merely natural gratitude to God. This can happen through wrong ideas about God, as if he were all love and mercy, and no avenging justice, or as if God were bound to love a person because of the person's worthiness. On these grounds men may love a God of their own imaginations, when they have no love at all for the true God.

Again, self-love can produce a love for God through a lack of conviction of sin. Some people have no sense of the vileness of sin, and no sense of God's infinite and holy opposition to it. They think God has no higher standards than they have! So they get on well with him and feel a sort of love for him, but they are loving an imaginary God, not the real God. Then there are others whose self-love produces a sort of love for God simply because of the material blessings they have received from his providence. There is nothing spiritual in this either!

Furthermore, others feel a vivid love for God because they believe strongly that God loves **them**. After going through great distress and fear of hell, they may suddenly come to believe that God loves them, has forgiven their sins and adopted them as his children. This may happen through an impression on their imaginations, or a voice speaking within them, or in some other unscriptural way. And if you asked these people whether God is lovely and excellent in himself, they might well say yes. However, the truth is that their good opinion of God was purchased by the great blessings they imagine they have received from him. They allow God to be lovely in himself, only because he has forgiven and accepted **them**, loves **them** so much, and has promised to take **them** to heaven. It is easy for them to love God and to say he is lovely, when they believe this. Anything is lovely to a selfish person if it advances his self-interest.

True spiritual love for God arises in Christians in a quite

different way. Real Christians do not first see that God loves **them**, and later on find out that he is lovely. They first see that God is lovely, that Christ is excellent and glorious. Their hearts are first captivated by this view of God, and their love for God arises chiefly from this view. True love begins with God and loves him for his own sake. Self-love begins with self, and loves God in the interests of self.

However, I would not want anyone to think that all gratitude to God for his blessings is a merely natural selfish thing. There is such a thing as spiritual gratitude. True spiritual gratitude differs from mere self-interested gratitude in the following ways:

(i) True gratitude to God for his blessings flows out of a love for God as he is in himself. The Christian has seen the glory of God, and it has captivated his heart. So his heart becomes tender and is easily touched when this glorious God gives him favours and blessings. I can illustrate this from human life. If a man has no love for another person, he can still feel thankful for some act of kindness done to him by that person. Even so, this is different from a man's gratitude to a beloved friend, for whom his heart already had a great affection. When our friends help us, it increases the love we already felt for them. Likewise, a love of God for his beauty and glory inclines us to still more love when this great God bestows blessings on us. So we cannot exclude all self-love from spiritual gratitude. 'I love the Lord, because he has heard my voice and my supplications' (Psalm 116:1). Nevertheless, our love for what God is prepares the way for our gratitude for what he does.

(ii) In spiritual gratitude, God's goodness touches people's hearts not just because it blesses **them**, but because God's goodness is part of the glory and beauty of his very nature. The incomparable grace of God revealed in the work of redemption, and shining in the face of Christ, is infinitely glorious in itself. The Christian sees this glory and delights in it. His personal interest in Christ's work, as a sinner needing salvation, helps to focus his mind on it. The sight of God's goodness acting for **his** redemption makes him pay all the more attention to God's glorious nature of goodness. So self-love becomes the servant of spiritual contemplation.

Some people might object to everything I have said by quoting 1 John 4:19, 'We love him because he first loved us.' They think this means that our **knowledge** of God's love for us is what first causes us to love God. I disagree. I think John means something quite different. He means that our love for God is something God puts in our hearts, as a token of **his** love to us. We love him, because he graciously inclines our hearts to love him; and he does this because of his free and sovereign love for us, by which he eternally chose us to become his lovers. In this sense, we love him because he first loved us. It is equivalent to saying, 'We are saved because he loved us when we had no love for him.'

I do admit there are other ways in which we love God because he first loved us, but this must refer to a spiritual love for God, not a mere selfish love. For example, God's love for sinners in Jesus Christ is one of the chief revelations of his glorious moral perfections. So God's love for us produces in us a love for God's moral perfection. Again, God's love for a particular elect person, revealed in that person's conversion, is a great display of God's glory to that person. So it produces holy spiritual gratitude, as explained above. In these ways, we love God with a holy and spiritual love because he first loved us. Why should we not assume that this is the kind of love for God that 1 John 4:19 is talking about, rather than a mere selfish love?

So far I have been discussing a Christian's **love** for God. What I have said applies equally to a Christian's **joy** and **delight** in God. Spiritual delight in God arises chiefly from his beauty and perfection, not from the blessings he gives us. Even the way of salvation through Christ is delightful chiefly because of its glorious exhibition of God's perfections. Of course the Christian rejoices that Christ is his personal Saviour. Still, this is not the deepest cause of his joy.

How different it is with false Christians! When they hear of God's love in sending his Son, Christ's love in dying for sinners, and the great blessings Christ has purchased and promised to his people, they may listen with great pleasure and feel highly elated. Yet if you examine their joy, you will find they are rejoicing because these blessings are **theirs**, all this exalts **them**. They can even delight in the doctrine of election, because it flatters their self-love to think they are heaven's favourites! Their joy is really a joy in themselves, not a joy in God.

So in all the joys of false Christians, their eyes are on themselves. Their minds are occupied with their own experiences, not the glory of God or the beauty of Christ. They keep thinking, 'What a good experience this is! What great revelations I am receiving! What a good story I now have to tell others!' So they put their experiences in the place of Christ. Instead of rejoicing in Christ's beauty and fulness, they rejoice in their wonderful experiences. And this shows itself in their talk. They are great talkers about themselves. The true Christian, when he feels spiritually warm and lively, loves to speak of God and Christ and the glorious truths of the gospel. False Christians are full of talk about themselves, the wonderful experiences **they** have had, how sure they are that God loves **them**, how safe **their** souls are, how they know **they** will go to heaven, etc.

3.
Spiritual emotions are based on the moral excellence of spiritual things.

What do I mean by the moral excellence of spiritual things?

I am not referring to what many people mean by 'morality'. Many use the word to refer to the mere outward performance of duties. Others use it to refer to the unspiritually motivated virtues an unbeliever can have — honesty, justice, generosity, etc. When I speak of moral excellence, what I mean is the sort of excellence that belongs to God's moral character. In other words, I am talking about the **holiness** of God. God's holiness is the sum total of his moral perfections — his righteousness, truth and goodness. (God does have other attributes, such as power, knowledge and eternity, but we do not call these **moral** attributes, because they are not qualities of God's **character**.)

I have already shown that spiritual emotions arise out of the loveliness of spiritual things. I am now going one step further, and stating that this loveliness is a moral loveliness. What a true Christian loves about spiritual things is their holiness. He loves God for the beauty of his holiness.

I do not mean that Christians see no loveliness in God's power, knowledge and eternity. However, we love these things for the sake of God's holiness. Power and knowledge do not make a being lovely without holiness. Who would see loveliness in a wicked man, just because he had great power and knowledge? It is holiness that makes these other qualities lovely. God's wisdom is glorious because it is a holy wisdom, not a wicked craftiness. God's eternity is glorious because it is a holy eternity, not an unchanging evil.

So love for God must begin with delight in his holiness, rather than in his other attributes. It is from God's holiness that the rest of his being derives its beauty. We will not see anything beautiful in God's knowledge, power, eternity, or other attributes, unless we first see the pure loveliness of his holiness.

As holiness is the beauty of God's nature, so it is the beauty of all spiritual things. The beauty of Christianity is that it is such a holy religion. The beauty of the Bible is the holiness of its teachings (Psalm 19:7-10). The beauty of our Lord Jesus is the holiness of his person — the 'holy one of God' (Acts 3:14). The beauty of the gospel is that it is a holy gospel, shining forth from the beauty of God and Jesus Christ. The beauty of heaven is its perfect holiness — the 'holy city' (Revelation 21:10).

I said before that God gives Christians a new spiritual sense. Now I can tell you exactly what this spiritual sense sees and feels and tastes. It is **the beauty of holiness**. Unbelievers cannot see this beauty, but the Holy Spirit has made Christians conscious of it.

Scripture points to the beauty of holiness as the true object of a spiritual appetite. This was the sweet food of the Lord Jesus Christ. 'I have food to eat of which you do not know. My food is to do the will of him who sent me, and to finish his work' (John 4:32 & 34). Then there is Psalm 119, one of the clearest passages in Scripture about the nature of true religion. It celebrates God's law, which reveals his holiness. It declares throughout that the excellence of this law is the chief object of a spiritual taste (eg. verses 14, 72, 103, 127, 131, 162). We find the same in Psalm 19 too, where the psalmist declares that God's holy laws are 'more to be desired than gold, yea, than much fine gold; sweeter also than honey and the honeycomb' (v. 10).

A spiritual person loves holy things for the same reason that an unspiritual person hates them — and what an unspiritual person hates about holy things is precisely their holiness! So, too, it is the holiness of holy things that a spiritual person loves. We see this in the saints and angels in heaven. What captivates their minds and hearts is the glory and beauty of God's holiness. 'And one cried to another and said, "Holy, holy, holy is the Lord of hosts; the whole earth is full of his glory!"' (Isaiah 6:3). 'And they do not rest day or night, saying: "Holy, holy, holy, Lord God Almighty, who was and is and is to come!"' (Revelation 4:8). 'Who shall not fear you, O Lord, and glorify your name? For you alone are holy' (Revelation 15:4). And as it is in heaven, so it should be on earth. 'Exalt the Lord our God, and worship at his footstool; for he is holy' (Psalm 99:5).

We can test our longings for heaven by this rule. Do we want to be there because of the holy beauty of God that shines there? Or is our desire for heaven based on a mere craving for selfish happiness?

4.
Spiritual emotions arise out of spiritual understanding.

Spiritual emotions are not heat without light. They arise out of spiritual illumination. The true Christian **feels**, because he **sees** and **understands** something more of spiritual things than he did before. He has a clearer and better view than he had before; either he receives some fresh understanding of God's truth, or he recovers a knowledge he once had but lost. 'And this I pray, that your love may abound still more and more in knowledge and all discernment' (Philippians 1:9). 'Put on the new man who is renewed in knowledge according to the image of him who created him' (Colossians 3:10).

At this point I want to emphasise that there is a great difference between **doctrinal** knowledge and **spiritual** knowledge. Doctrinal knowledge involves the intellect alone, but spiritual knowledge is a **sense of the heart** by which we see the beauty of holiness in Christian doctrines. Spiritual knowledge always involves the intellect and the heart together. We need to understand what a Scripture doctrine means intellectually, and to taste the holy beauty of that meaning with our hearts.

A person can have great knowledge of doctrines in his intellect, and yet have no taste for the beauty of holiness in those doctrines. He knows intellectually in his head, but he does not know spiritually in his heart. Mere doctrinal knowledge is like a person who has looked at and touched honey. Spiritual knowledge is like a person who has felt the sweet taste of honey on his lips. He knows much more about honey than a person who has only looked at it and touched it!

It follows that a spiritual understanding of Scripture does not mean an understanding of its parables, types and allegories. A person might know how to interpret all these things, without having a single ray of spiritual light in his soul. 'Though I have the gift of prophecy, and understand all mysteries and all knowledge, but have not love, I am nothing' (1 Corinthians 13:2). The 'spiritual meaning' of Scripture is the divine sweetness of its truths, not the correct interpretation of its symbolic passages.

Again, it would not be spiritual knowledge if God immediately revealed his will to our minds by the Holy Spirit. Such knowledge would still only be doctrinal, not spiritual. Facts about God's will are doctrines, just as much as facts about God's nature and works! So we would still be dealing with mere doctrinal knowledge, even supposing God did reveal his will directly to our minds. Immediate revelations could not make our knowledge spiritual, if we had no sense of the holy beauty of God's will.

There is another common error about spiritual understanding I want to correct. Some people claim that God reveals his will to them by impressing a text of Scripture on their minds —

often a text about a Bible character and his conduct. For example, a Christian is trying to decide whether to go to a foreign land, where he is likely to encounter many difficulties and dangers. God's words to Jacob in Genesis 46:4 come powerfully into his mind: 'I will go down with you into Egypt, and I will surely bring you up again.' These words relate to Jacob and his conduct, but the Christian interprets them as referring to himself. He interprets 'Egypt' as the foreign country he has in mind, and thinks God is promising to take him there and bring him back again safely. He might call this a 'spiritual understanding' of the text, or the Holy Spirit applying it to him.

However, there is nothing spiritual about this. Spiritual understanding sees what is actually in Scripture; it does not make a new meaning for it. Making a new meaning for Scripture is equivalent to making a new Scripture! It is adding to God's Word, a practice God condemns (Proverbs 30:6). The true spiritual meaning of Scripture is the meaning it originally had when the Spirit first inspired it. This original meaning is what everybody would see, if they were not spiritually blind.

No doubt these experiences arouse vivid emotions. Of course people feel very moved when they think God is guiding them by a text in this way, or directly revealing his will to them by his Spirit. My point, however, is this: none of these experiences consists in a sense or taste of the beauty of God's holiness. And emotions are spiritual only when they arise out of this spiritual sight of the loveliness of God's holiness. If emotions arise merely out of suggestions in the mind, or words coming into the head, they are not spiritual in nature.

A large part of the false religion in the world is made up of these experiences and the false emotions they excite. Non-Christian religions are full of them. So (unfortunately) is the history of the Church. These experiences captivate people, especially the less intelligent; they think that these impressions, visions and raptures are what Christianity is all about. So Satan transforms himself into an angel of light, deceives multitudes, and corrupts true religion. Church leaders must be constantly on their guard against these delusions, especially during times of revival.

Before moving on, I want to make one thing clear. I do not want anyone to misunderstand what I have said. I am not saying that emotions are unspiritual just because imaginary ideas go along with them. Human nature is such that we cannot think intensely about anything without having imaginary ideas of some sort. Nevertheless, if our emotions **arise out of** these imaginary ideas, and not out of spiritual knowledge, then our emotions are spiritually worthless. I want people to keep this distinction in mind: **imaginary ideas can arise out of spiritual emotions, but spiritual emotions cannot arise out of imaginary ideas**. Spiritual emotions can only arise out of spiritual knowledge, the sense of the heart which sees the beauty of holiness. And if imaginary ideas accompany a truly spiritual emotion, they are not essential to it, but an accidental effect.

5. Spiritual emotions bring a conviction of the reality of divine things.

Remember the Scripture text at the beginning of this book: 'Though you have not seen him, you love him, and though you do not see him now, but believe in him, you greatly rejoice with joy inexpressible and full of glory' (1 Peter 1:8, NASB).

The true Christian has a solid, effective conviction of the truth of the gospel. He no longer hesitates between two opinions. The gospel ceases to be doubtful or only probably true, and becomes settled and indisputable in his mind. The great, spiritual, mysterious and invisible things of the gospel influence his heart as powerful realities. He does not simply have an opinion that Jesus is the Son of God; God opens his eyes to **see** that this is the case. As to the things Jesus teaches about God, God's will, salvation and heaven, the Christian also knows that these things are undoubted realities. So they have a practical influence on his heart and his behaviour.

It is obvious from Scripture that all true Christians have this conviction about divine things. I will mention just a few texts out of many: 'He said to them, "But who do you say that I am?" And Simon Peter answered and said, "You are the Christ, the Son of the living God." Jesus answered and said to him, "Blessed are you, Simon Bar-Jonah, for flesh and blood has not revealed this to you, but my Father who is in heaven"' (Matthew 16:15-17). 'I have manifested your name to the men whom you have given me out of the world. They were yours, you gave them to me, and they have kept your word. Now they have known that all things which you have given me are from you. For I have given them the words which you have given me; and they have received them, and have known surely that I came forth from you; and they have believed that you sent me' (John 17:6-8). 'I know whom I have believed and am persuaded that he is able to keep what I have committed to him until that day' (2 Timothy 1:12). 'We have known and believed the love that God has for us' (1 John 4:16).

There are many religious experiences which fail to bring this conviction. Many so-called revelations are **moving** but not **convincing**. They produce no lasting change in a person's attitude and conduct. There are people who have such experiences, yet in their daily lives they do not act under the practical influence of a conviction of infinite, eternal realities. Their emotions blaze up for a while, then die away again, leaving behind no lasting conviction.

However, let us suppose that a person's religious emotions do arise from a strong conviction that Christianity is true. Are his emotions spiritual? No, not necessarily. In fact, his emotions are still unspiritual, unless his conviction is **reasonable**. By a 'reasonable conviction', I mean a conviction founded on real evidence and good reasons. People of other faiths can have a strong conviction of the truth of their religion. Often they accept their religion merely because their parents and neighbours and nation believe it. If a professing Christian has no other basis for his faith than this, his religion is no better than that of anyone else who believes merely on the grounds of his upbringing. No doubt the **truth** the Christian believes is better, but if his **belief** in that truth comes only from his upbringing, then the belief itself is on the same level as that of people of other religions. The emotions that flow from such a belief are no better than the religious emotions found in other faiths.

Furthermore, let us suppose a person's belief in Christianity is not based on his upbringing, but on reasons and arguments. Are his emotions now spiritual? Again, not necessarily. Unspiritual emotions can arise even from a reasonable belief. The belief itself has to be **spiritual** as well as reasonable. The fact is that rational arguments will sometimes convince a person intellectually that Christianity is true, and yet that person remains unsaved. Simon the magician believed intellectually (Acts 8:13), but he remained 'poisoned by bitterness and bound by iniquity' (Acts 8:23). Intellectual belief can certainly produce emotions, as in the demons who 'believe and tremble' (James 2:19), but such emotions are not spiritual.

Spiritual conviction of the truth arises only in a spiritual person. It is only when God's Spirit enlightens our minds to understand spiritual realities, that we can have a spiritual conviction of their truth. Remember, spiritual understanding means an inward sense of the holy beauty of divine things. I will now describe how this understanding convinces us of the reality of these things.

God is unique. He is utterly different from all other beings, and it is God's beauty, more than any other divine attribute, which sets him apart. This beauty is utterly different from all other beauty. So when the Christian sees this beauty in Christianity, he sees God in it. He sees the divine beauty which is the chief distinguishing feature of God. This gives the Christian a direct, intuitive knowledge that Christ's gospel comes from God. He does not need to be convinced by long complicated arguments. The argument is simple: he grasps the truth of the gospel because he sees its divine beauty and glory.

Many of the most important truths of the gospel depend on its spiritual beauty. Since the natural man cannot see this beauty, it is little wonder he does not believe these truths. Let me give some examples. Unless we see the beauty of holiness, we will be blind to the ugliness of sin. In consequence, we will not understand the way Scripture condemns sin. Nor will we understand what Scripture says about the terrible sinfulness of mankind. A person can only see and feel the desperate depravity of his own heart, if the Holy Spirit gives him this ability to taste the sweetness of holiness and the bitterness of sin. Only this convinces us that Scripture speaks truly about the corruption of human nature, man's need of a Saviour, and God's mighty power to change and renew the human heart. It also convinces us that God is just in punishing sin so severely, and that man cannot atone for his own sin. This sense of spiritual beauty enables the soul to see the glory of Christ as Scripture reveals him. We understand the infinite value of his atonement and the excellence of the gospel way of salvation. We see that man's happiness consists in holiness, and we feel the indescribable glory of heaven. The truth of all these things appears to the soul, only when it receives that spiritual sense of divine beauty I have been speaking of.

If conviction of the truth of the gospel cannot arise out of this sense of its divine beauty, most people will never have any belief in its truth. Scholars and academics can believe on the basis of historical evidence, but this is not available to most of us. Historical evidence requires a knowledge of many other historical writings outside of Scripture. By comparing these writings with Scripture, one can see how reliable Scripture is in its historical accounts of people and events. Even so, who is going to do this except scholars? If an unbeliever has to become a historian before he can become a Christian, how many will become Christians? Must we go through a long, laborious process of studying non-Scriptural historical writings, before we can believe Scripture? Has God really made it so difficult for us to come to a reasonable conviction of the truth of his gospel?

The fact is that very few people actually come to believe in this way. Large numbers of Christians in the past were illiterate, but they still believed, and believed rightly. Nor did their belief depend on what scholars and historians told them. If it had, it would have been a mere human opinion, rather than the full assurance God's Word demands. 'Let us draw near with a true heart in full assurance of faith' (Hebrews 10:22). 'That their hearts may be encouraged, being knit together in love, and attaining to all riches of the full assurance of understanding, to the knowledge of the mystery of God' (Colossians 2:2). We cannot obtain this kind of certainty from what scholars and historians tell us. Instead, God himself gives it to us. He opens our eyes to see the unspeakably beautiful and divine glory that shines in his gospel. We see God in it. This evidence is totally convincing. The natural man may be blind to it, as an uncultured person is blind to the beauty of great poetry. The spiritual Christian, however, sees and tastes and relishes this beautiful divine glory of the gospel, which melts away all his doubts and convinces him it is true.

I am not saying that every Christian feels the same degree of spiritual certainty all the time. We obtain assurance of the truth of the gospel as we see its divine beauty, but sometimes our sight of it becomes clouded. What we need is an ever clearer view of this divine beauty of Christianity, if our assurance is to be vivid and powerful.

Again, I am not saying that historical evidence and other arguments for Christianity are useless. We should value them highly. They can force unbelievers to take Christianity seriously. They can confirm the faith of believers. What they cannot do is produce spiritual certainty. Only a sight of the spiritual beauty and glory of divine things can do that.

6.
Spiritual emotions always exist alongside spiritual humiliation.

Spiritual humiliation is the sense a Christian has of how insufficient and detestable he is, which leads him to abase himself and exalt God alone. At the same time, there is another kind of humiliation, which we may call **legal** humiliation. Legal humiliation is an experience which only unbelievers can have. The law of God works on their consciences, and makes them realise how sinful and helpless they are. However, they do not see the hateful nature of sin, or renounce sin in their hearts, or surrender themselves to God. They feel humbled as if by force, but they have no humility. They feel what every wicked person and devil will feel on Judgment Day: convicted, humiliated, and forced to admit that God is in the right, but they remain unconverted.

Spiritual humiliation, by contrast, springs out of the true Christian's sense of the beauty and glory of God's holiness. It makes him feel how vile and contemptible he is in himself because of his sinfulness. It leads him to prostrate himself freely and gladly at God's feet, and to deny himself and renounce his sins.

Spiritual humiliation is of the essence of true religion. Those who lack it are not genuine Christians, no matter how wonderful their experiences may be. Scripture is very full in its testimony to the necessity of this humiliation: 'The Lord is near to those who have a broken heart, and saves such as have a contrite spirit' (Psalm 34:18). 'The sacrifices of God are a broken spirit, a broken and a contrite heart — these, O God, you will not despise' (Psalm 51:17). 'Thus says the Lord: "Heaven is my throne, and earth is my footstool ... But on this one will I look: on him who is poor and of a contrite spirit, and who trembles at my word"' (Isaiah 66:1-2). 'Blessed are the poor in spirit, for theirs is the kingdom of heaven' (Matthew 5:3). See also the parable of the Pharisee and the tax collector, Luke 18:9-14.

Spiritual humiliation is the essence of Christian self-denial. This consists in two parts. First, a man must deny his worldly inclinations, and forsake all sinful pleasures. Second, he must deny his natural self-righteousness and self-centredness. This second part is the hardest to do. Many have done the first without doing the second; they have rejected physical pleasures, only to enjoy the devilish pleasure of pride.

Of course, proud hypocrites pretend to be humble, but they generally make a bad job of it. Their humility usually consists in telling others how humble they are. They say things like, 'I am the least of all saints,' 'I am a poor vile creature,' 'My heart is worse than the devil,' etc. They say all this, and yet expect others to regard them as outstanding saints. If someone else said about a hypocrite what that hypocrite says about himself, how offended he would be!

Spiritual pride can be very subtle, disguising itself as humility, but there are two signs which betray it:

(i) The proud man compares himself with others in spiritual things, and has a superior opinion of himself. He is eager for leadership among God's people, and wishes his opinion to be everyone's law. He wants other Christians to look up to him and follow him in matters of religion.

The truly humble man is the opposite of this. His humility makes him think others better than himself (Philippians 2:3). It is not natural for him to take upon himself the office of teacher; he thinks others are better suited to it, as Moses did (Exodus 3:11-4:7). He is more eager to listen than to speak (James 1:19). And when he does speak, it is not in a bold, self-confident way, but with trembling. He does not enjoy exercising power over others, but would rather follow than lead.

(ii) Another sure sign of spiritual pride is that the proud man tends to think very highly of his humility, whereas the truly humble man thinks of himself as very proud!

This is because the proud man and the humble man have different views of themselves. We measure a man's humiliation by our view of his proper dignity and greatness. If a king knelt down to remove the shoe of another king, we would consider this an act of self-abasement, and so would the king who did it. By contrast, if a slave knelt down to remove the shoe of his king, nobody would think that a great act of self-abasement, or a sign of great humility. The slave himself would not think so, unless he were ridiculously conceited. If he went about afterwards, boasting about what great humility he had displayed in removing the king's shoe, everyone would laugh at him! 'Who do you think you are,' they would say, 'that you think it very humble of you to take off the king's shoe?'

The proud man is like the conceited slave. He thinks it a great sign of humility to confess his unworthiness before God. This is because he has such a high view of himself. How humble of **him** to confess his unworthiness! If he had a proper view of himself, he would rather feel astonished and ashamed that he was not more humbled before God.

The truly humble man never feels that he has sufficiently abased himself before God. He feels that however low he bends, he could bend lower. He always feels that he is above his proper position before God. He looks at his position, and looks at where he should be, and he appears at a great distance from it. He calls the distance 'pride'. It is his pride that appears to him to be great, not his humility. It does not seem to him to be a great sign of his humility that he should lie in the dust at the feet of God. He thinks that is exactly where he belongs.

Reader, do not forget to apply these things to yourself. Does it offend you when someone thinks himself a better Christian than everyone else? Do you think he is proud, and that you are humbler than he is? Then be careful, in case you become proud of your humility! Examine yourself. If you conclude, 'It seems to me that no-one is as sinful as I am,' do not be satisfied with this. Do you think you are better than others, because you admit that you are so sinful? Do you have a high opinion of this humility of yours? If you say, 'No, I do not have a high opinion of my humility, I think I am as proud as the devil,' then examine yourself again. Perhaps you are proud of the fact that you do not have a high opinion of your humility? You might be proud of admitting how proud you are!

7. Spiritual emotions always exist alongside a change of nature.

All spiritual emotions arise from a spiritual understanding, in which the soul sees the excellence and glory of divine things. This spiritual sight has a transforming effect. 'But we all, with unveiled face, beholding as in a mirror the glory of the Lord, are being transformed into the same image from glory to glory, just as by the Spirit of the Lord' (2 Corinthians 3:18). This transforming power comes only from God — from the Spirit of the Lord.

Scripture describes conversion in terms which imply or signify a change of nature: being born again, becoming new creatures, rising from the dead, being renewed in the spirit of the mind, dying to sin and living to righteousness, putting off the old man and putting on the new, becoming partakers of the divine nature, and so on.

It follows that if there is no real and lasting change in people who think they are converted, their religion is worthless, whatever their experiences may be. Conversion is the turning of the whole man from sin to God. God can restrain unconverted people from sin, of course, but in conversion he turns the very heart and nature from sin to holiness. The converted person becomes the enemy of sin. What, then, shall we make of a person who says he has experienced conversion, but whose religious emotions soon die away, leaving him much the same person as he was before? He seems as selfish, worldly, foolish, perverse and un-Christian as ever. This speaks **against** him louder than any religious experiences can speak **for** him. In Christ Jesus, neither circumcision nor uncircumcision, neither a dramatic experience nor a quiet one, neither a wonderful testimony nor a dull one, counts for anything. The only thing that counts is a new creation.

Of course, we must make allowances for the natural temperament of individuals. Conversion does not destroy natural temperament. If our temperament made us prone to certain sins before our conversion, we may very possibly be prone to the same sins after conversion. Nevertheless, conversion will make a difference even here. Though God's grace does not destroy the failings of temperament, it can correct them. If a man before his conversion was inclined by his natural temperament to lust, drunkenness or revenge, his conversion will have a powerful effect on these evil inclinations. He may still be in danger from these sins more than any others, but they will not dominate his soul and his life as they did before. They will no longer be part of his true character. In fact, sincere repentance will make a person particularly hate and fear the sins of which he used to be most guilty.

8.
True spiritual emotions differ from false ones, in promoting a Christlike spirit of love, humility, peace, forgiveness and compassion.

All real disciples of Christ have this spirit in them. It is the spirit which so possesses and dominates them, that it is their true and proper character. Christ makes this clear in the sermon on the mount, when he describes the character of those who are truly blessed: 'Blessed are the meek, for they shall inherit the earth. Blessed are the merciful, for they shall obtain mercy. Blessed are the peacemakers, for they shall be called sons of God' (Matthew 5:5,7,9). The apostle Paul tells us that this spirit is the special character of God's elect: 'Therefore, as the elect of God, holy and beloved, put on tender mercies, kindness, humbleness of mind, meekness, long-suffering; bearing with one another, and forgiving one another' (Colossians 3:12-13). James teaches the same: 'But if you have bitter envy and self-seeking in your hearts, do not boast and lie against the truth. This wisdom does not descend from above, but is earthly, sensual, demonic. For where envy and self-seeking exist, confusion and every evil thing will be there. But the wisdom that is from above is first pure, then peaceful, gentle, willing to yield, full of mercy and good fruits' (James 3:14-17).

Holiness in all its aspects belongs to the Christian character. Even so, there are certain aspects of holiness which deserve the name of 'Christian' in a special degree, because they reflect the divine attributes which God and Christ particularly displayed in redeeming sinners. The qualities I have in mind are humility, gentleness, love, forgiveness and mercy.

Scripture particularly points to these qualities in the character of Christ. 'Learn from me, for I am gentle and lowly in heart' (Matthew 11:29). These qualities shine out in that title of Christ, 'the Lamb'. The great shepherd of the sheep is himself a lamb, and he calls believers his lambs. 'Feed my lambs' (John 21:15). 'I send you out as lambs among wolves' (Luke 10:3). Christians follow Christ as the Lamb. 'These are the ones who follow the Lamb wherever he goes' (Revelation 14:4). If we follow the Lamb of God, we must imitate his gentleness and humility.

Scripture holds out the same qualities under the symbol of the dove. When the Spirit of Holiness descended on Christ at his baptism, it descended on him like a dove. The dove is a symbol of gentleness, innocence, love and peace. The same Spirit that descended on the head of the Church descends on the members too. 'God has sent forth the Spirit of his Son into your hearts' (Galatians 4:6). 'If anyone does not have the Spirit of Christ, he is not his' (Romans 8:9). 'There is one body and one Spirit' (Ephesians 4:4). It follows that true Christians will exhibit the same dove-like qualities of gentleness, peace and love which characterised Jesus.

I can hear someone objecting at this point, 'What about Christian boldness, and being bold for Christ, and being good soldiers in the Christian warfare, and making a stand against the enemies of Christ and his people?'

There is indeed such a thing as Christian courage and boldness. The most outstanding Christians are the greatest warriors, and have a brave and intrepid spirit. It is our duty as Christians to be vigorous and resolute in opposing those who try to overthrow Christ's kingdom and the cause of his gospel. However, many people totally misunderstand the nature of this

Christian boldness. It is not a brutal fierceness. Christian boldness consists of two things: (i) ruling and suppressing the evil emotions of the mind; (ii) resolutely following and acting on the mind's good emotions, without being hindered by sinful fear or the hostility of enemies. And although this boldness appears in withstanding our outward enemies, it appears much more in resisting and conquering the enemies within us. The courage and resolution of the Christian soldier appear most gloriously when he maintains a holy calmness and humility and love against all the storms, injuries, strange behaviour and disturbing events of an evil and unreasonable world. 'He who is slow to anger is better than the mighty, and he who rules his spirit than he who takes a city' (Proverbs 16:32).

There is a false boldness for Christ which arises from pride. It is the nature of spiritual pride to want to stand out from others. So men will often oppose those whom they call 'carnal', simply to gain the admiration of their own party. True boldness for Christ, however, lifts the believer above the displeasure of friends and foes alike. He will rather offend all parties than offend Christ. In fact, boldness for Christ appears more clearly when a man is ready to lose the admiration of his own party, than when he opposes enemies with his party behind him. The truly intrepid Christian is brave enough to confess a fault to his enemies, if conscience requires it. It takes more spiritual courage to do this than to oppose enemies fiercely!

Let me say something about the Christian spirit as it appears in these three things — forgiveness, love and mercy. Scripture is quite clear about the absolute necessity of these qualities in the character of every Christian.

A **forgiving** spirit is a readiness to forgive others the harm they do to us. Christ teaches that if we have this spirit, it is a sign that we are in a state of forgiveness ourselves. On the other hand, if we lack this spirit, God has not forgiven us. 'And forgive us our debts, as we forgive our debtors ... For if you forgive men their trespasses, your heavenly Father will also forgive you. But if you do not forgive men their trespasses, neither will your Father forgive your trespasses' (Matthew 6:12, 14-15).

Scripture is very plain that all true Christians have a **loving** spirit. It is the quality that Scripture insists on more than any other, as a sign of genuine Christianity. 'This is my commandment, that you love one another as I have loved you' (John 15:12). 'By this all will know that you are my disciples, if you have love for one another' (John 13:35). 'Beloved, let us love one another, for love is of God; and everyone who loves is born of God and knows God. He who does not love does not know God, for God is love' (1 John 4:7-8). 'Though I speak with the tongues of men and angels, but have not love, I have become as sounding brass or a clanging cymbal. And though I have the gift of prophecy, and understand all mysteries and all knowledge, and though I have all faith, so that I could remove mountains, but have not love, I am nothing' (1 Corinthians 13:1-2).

Scripture is also clear that only those who have a **merciful** spirit are true Christians. A merciful spirit is a disposition to pity and help our fellow men when they are needy or suffering. 'The righteous shows mercy and gives' (Psalm 37:21). 'He who honours God has mercy on the needy' (Proverbs 14:31). 'If a brother or sister is naked and destitute of daily food, and one of you says to them, "Depart in peace, be warmed and filled," but you do not give them the things which are needed for the body, what does it profit?' (James 2:15-16).

Do not misunderstand me. I do not mean that in the true Christian there is nothing contrary to the spirit I have described above. The Christian is not sinlessly perfect. Even so, I do say that wherever true Christianity is at work, it will have this tendency and promote this spirit. Scripture knows nothing of true Christians who have a selfish, angry, quarrelsome spirit. No matter what a person's religious experiences may be, he has no right to think himself truly converted if his spirit is under the control of bitterness and spite. All real Christians are under the government of the lamb-like, dove-like spirit of Jesus Christ. All true spiritual emotions nurture this spirit.

9.
True spiritual emotions soften the heart, and exist alongside a Christian tenderness of spirit.

False emotions may seem to melt the heart for a time, but in the end they harden it. People under the influence of false emotions eventually become less concerned about their sins — their past, present and future sins. They take less notice of the warnings of God's Word and the chastenings of his providence. They become more careless about the state of their souls and the manner of their behaviour. They become less discerning about what is sinful, and less afraid of the appearance of evil in what they say and do. Why? Because they have such a high opinion of themselves. They have had religious impressions and experiences. So they think they are safe. When they were under conviction of sin and fear of hell, they may have been very conscientious in the duties of religion and morality. However, now that they think they are no longer in danger of hell, they begin to forsake self-denial, and allow themselves to indulge in their various lusts.

Such people do not accept Christ as their Saviour **from** sin. They trust in him as the Saviour **of** their sins! They think Christ will allow them the quiet enjoyment of their sins, and protect them from God's displeasure. Jude speaks about such people as 'certain men who have crept in unawares ... who turn the grace of our God into licentiousness' (Jude 4). God himself warns us against this error: 'When I say to the righteous that he shall surely live, but he trusts in his own righteousness and commits iniquity, none of his righteous works shall be remembered; but because of the iniquity that he has committed, he shall die' (Ezekiel 33:13).

True spiritual emotions have the opposite effect. They turn a heart of stone more and more into a heart of flesh. They make the heart tender, like bruised flesh which is easily hurt. Christ points to this tenderness by speaking of the true Christian as a little child (Matthew 10:42 and 18:3, John 13:33). The flesh of a little child is tender. So is the heart of a spiritually new-born person. And not only the flesh, but the mind of a little child is also tender. A little child easily feels sympathy and cannot bear to see others in distress. So it is with a Christian. Kindness easily wins the affection of a little child. So it is with a Christian. A little child easily becomes afraid at the appearance of outward evils. So a Christian becomes alarmed at the appearance of moral evil. When a little child meets anything threatening, it does not trust in its own strength, but runs to its parents. So a Christian is not self-confident in fighting spiritual enemies, but runs to Christ. A little child easily feels suspicious of danger in the dark, when alone, or far from home. So a Christian becomes aware of spiritual dangers, and feels concerned for his soul, when he cannot see his way clear before him; he is afraid of being left alone and at a distance from God. A little child easily feels afraid of his elders, fears their anger and trembles at their threats. So a Christian fears to offend God and trembles at God's chastening.

In all these ways a true Christian resembles a little child. In spiritual things, the tallest and strongest saint is the smallest and tenderest child.

10.
True spiritual emotions, unlike false ones, have a beautiful symmetry and balance.

The symmetry of the Christian's virtues is not perfect in this life. It is often imperfect, through lack of teaching, errors of judgment, the power of natural temperament, and many other factors. Even so, true Christians never display that grotesque lack of balance which marks the religion of hypocrites.

Let me give a particular example of what I mean. In the true Christian, joy and comfort go along with godly sorrow and mourning for sin. We never feel any godly sorrow until we become new creatures in Christ, and one of the signs of the true Christian is that he mourns, and continues to mourn, for sin, 'Blessed are those who mourn, for they shall be comforted' (Matthew 5:4). The joy of salvation and a godly sorrow for sin go together in true religion. On the other hand, many hypocrites rejoice without trembling.

Hypocrites also display a grotesque lack of balance in their attitudes to different persons and objects. Take, for instance, the way in which they exercise love. Some make a great show of their love for God and Christ, but they are quarrelsome, envious, vindictive and slanderous towards their fellow men. This is sheer hypocrisy! 'If someone says, "I love God," and hates his brother, he is a liar; for he who does not love his brother whom he has seen, how can he love God whom he has not seen?' (1 John 4:20). On the other hand, there are people who seem very warm and friendly and helpful to their fellow men — but they have no love for God!

Again, there are people who love those who agree with them and admire them, but have no time for those who oppose and dislike them. A Christian's love must be universal! 'Be sons of your Father in heaven; for he makes his sun rise on the evil and on the good, and sends rain on the just and unjust. For if you love those who love you, what reward have you? Do not even the tax collectors do the same?' (Matthew 5:45-6).

Some people show love to others in respect of their bodily needs, but have no love for their souls. Others pretend a great love for men's souls, but have no compassion for their bodies. (To make a great show of pity and distress for souls often costs nothing; to show mercy to men's bodies, we have to part with our money!) True Christian love extends both to the souls and to the bodies of our neighbours. This is what Christ's compassion was like, as we see in Mark 6:34-44. His compassion for the people's souls moved him to teach them, and his compassion for their bodies moved him to feed them by the miracle of the five loaves and two fish.

You see from all this what I mean when I say that false religion is unbalanced and devoid of symmetry. We can see this lack of balance in many other ways. Some, for instance, get very agitated over the sins of their fellow Christians, but do not seem very troubled about their own sins. A true Christian, however, feels more concerned over his own sins than the sins of other people. He will of course be upset when his fellow Christians sin, but he is always quicker to detect and condemn his own sins. Then there are those who show a zeal for spiritual leadership, but no corresponding zeal for prayer. Others feel warm religious emotions when in the company of Christians, but grow cold in solitude, etc.

11. True spiritual emotions produce a longing for deeper holiness, but false emotions rest satisfied in themselves.

The more a true Christian loves God, the more he desires to love him, and the more uneasy he is at his lack of love for him. The more a true Christian hates sin, the more he desires to hate it, and grieves that he still loves it so much. The most that Christians have in this life is only a foretaste of their future glory. The most outstanding believer is only a child compared with what he shall be in heaven. This is why the greatest degrees of holiness believers reach in this world do not quench their desires after more. On the contrary, they become more eager to press forwards. 'One thing I do, forgetting those things which are behind and reaching forward to those things which are ahead, I press towards the goal for the prize of the upward call of God in Christ Jesus. Therefore let us, as many as are mature, have this mind' (Philippians 3:13-15).

Someone may object, 'How is this ceaseless striving consistent with the satisfaction that spiritual enjoyment brings?'

There is no inconsistency here. Spiritual enjoyment satisfies the soul in the following respects:

(i) Spiritual enjoyment is perfectly adapted to the nature and needs of the human soul. The person who has this enjoyment never wearies of it. It is his deepest joy, and he would never exchange it for any other. That does not mean, however, that a person who experiences something of spiritual enjoyment desires no more of the same.

(ii) Spiritual enjoyment lives up to our expectations. Great desire produces great anticipation. When we receive some worldly joy we have greatly desired, it often disappoints us, but not so with spiritual enjoyments! They always live up to our expectations.

(iii) Spiritual enjoyment satisfies the soul to the degree that the soul is capable of receiving satisfaction. Even so, there is room for the soul's capacity to expand infinitely. If we are not as spiritually satisfied as we could be, the fault lies in us. We are not opening our mouths wide enough.

Spiritual enjoyment, then, does satisfy the soul in these respects. It meets our deepest need, lives up to our expectations, and fills us according to our capacity to receive. All this is perfectly consistent with ever thirsting for more and more of the same, until our enjoyment becomes perfect.

It is different with false religious joys. When convicted of sin and afraid of hell, a person might long for spiritual light, faith in Christ, love for God. When false experiences have deceived him into thinking he is saved, he rests content with this. He no longer desires grace and holiness, especially if his experiences have been very impressive. He does not live for God and Christ in the present, but lives off his conversion in the past.

The true Christian is totally different. He is constantly seeking God. In fact, 'those who seek God' is one of the ways the Bible describes genuine believers. 'The humble shall see this and be glad; and you who seek God, your hearts shall live' (Psalm 69:32). 'Let all those who seek you rejoice and be glad in you' (Psalm 70:4). Scripture depicts the seeking and striving of the Christian as occurring mainly **after** his conversion. Scripture is speaking about those who are already Christians when it talks of running the race, wrestling with principalities and powers, pressing forward, continuing in prayer, crying to God day and night. Sadly, many people today have fallen into an unscriptural way of speaking, as if all their wrestling and striving were before their conversion, and now as Christians everything is peaceful and easy.

Doubtless some hypocrites will say that they do constantly seek more of God and Christ and holiness, but a hypocrite does not really seek spiritual things for their own sake. He always has a self-centred reason. He wants better spiritual experiences for the sake of the selfish assurance they bring, or because they flatter him as a favourite of God. He wants to feel God's love for himself, rather than to have more love for God. Because he knows a real Christian is supposed to have certain desires, he imitates them. However, a longing for experiences, or for a feeling of God's love, or for death and heaven, are not the most reliable signs of a true Christian. The best sign is a longing for a holier heart and a holier life.

12.
The fruit of true spiritual emotions is Christian practice.

Christian practice means three things:

(i) The true Christian directs all aspects of his behaviour by Christian rules.

(ii) He makes holy living the main concern of his life. It is his work and business above all other things.

(iii) He perseveres in this business constantly, to the end of his life.

Let us establish these three points from Scripture.

(i) The true Christian seeks to conform every single area of his life to the rules of God's Word. 'You are my friends if you do whatever I command you' (John 15:14). 'And everyone who has this hope in him purifies himself, just as Christ is pure ... Little children, let no-one deceive you. He who practises righteousness is righteous, just as Christ is righteous' (1 John 3:3 & 7). 'Do you not know that the unrighteous will not inherit the kingdom of God? Do not be deceived. Neither fornicators, nor idolaters, nor adulterers, nor homosexuals, nor sodomites, nor thieves, nor covetous, nor drunkards, nor revilers, nor extortioners will inherit the kingdom of God' (1 Corinthians 6:9-10). 'Now the works of the flesh are evident, which are: adultery, fornication, uncleanness, licentiousness, idolatry, sorcery, hatred, contentions, jealousies, outbursts of wrath, selfish ambitions, dissensions, heresies, envy, murders, drunkenness, revels, and the like; of which I tell you beforehand, just as I told you in time past, that those who practise such things will not inherit the kingdom of God' (Galatians 5:19-21).

This commitment to total obedience does not mean a mere negative avoidance of evil practices. It also means positively obeying God's commands. We cannot say that someone is a true Christian just because he is **not** a thief, liar, blasphemer, drunkard, sexually immoral, arrogant, cruel or fierce. He also has to be positively God-fearing, humble, respectful, gentle, peaceful, forgiving, merciful and loving. Without these positive qualities, he is not obeying the laws of Christ.

(ii) The true Christian makes holy living the main business of his life. Christ's people not only do good works, they are **zealous** for good works (Titus 2:14). God has not called us to idleness, but to work and labour for him. All true Christians are good and faithful soldiers of Jesus Christ (2 Timothy 2:3). They fight the good fight of faith in order to lay hold on eternal life (1 Timothy 6:12). Those who run in a race all run, but only one receives the prize; lazy and negligent people are not running so as to obtain that prize (1 Corinthians 9:24). The true Christian puts on the whole armour of God, without which he cannot withstand the fiery darts of the devil (Ephesians 6:13-17). He forgets the things which are behind, and reaches forward to the things which are ahead, pressing towards the goal, since this is the only way to obtain the prize of the upward call of God in Christ Jesus (Philippians 3:13-14). Laziness in serving God is as damning as open rebellion; the lazy servant is a wicked servant, and will be cast into outer darkness with God's open enemies (Matthew 25:26 & 30).

This shows that a real Christian is one who is diligent, earnest and committed in his religion. As Hebrews puts it, 'we desire that each one of you show the same diligence to the full assurance of hope until the end, that you do not become sluggish, but imitate those who through faith and patience inherit the promises' (Hebrews 6:11-12).

(iii) The true Christian perseveres in his obedience to God throughout all the difficulties he meets, to the end of his life. Scripture teaches very fully that true faith perseveres; see, for example, the parable of the sower (Matthew 13:3-9, 18-23).

The central thing Scripture emphasises in the doctrine of perseverance, is that the genuine Christian keeps on believing and obeying despite the various **problems** he meets. God allows these problems to come into the lives of people who claim to be Christians, to test the reality of their faith. It then becomes clear to themselves, and often to others, whether they really mean business with Christ. These problems are sometimes spiritual, such as a particularly enticing temptation. Sometimes the difficulties are outward, such as the insults and ridicule and loss of possessions to which our Christianity might expose us. The sign of the genuine Christian is that he perseveres through these problems and difficulties, and remains true to Christ.

Here are some texts which relate to this. 'For you, O God, have proved us; you have refined us as silver is refined. You brought us into the net; you laid affliction on our backs. You have caused men to ride over our heads; we went through fire and through water; but you brought us out to rich fulfilment' (Psalm 66:10-12). 'Blessed is the man who endures temptation; for when he has been proved, he will receive the crown of life which the Lord has promised to those who love him' (James 1:12). 'Do not fear any of those things which you are about to suffer. Indeed, the devil is about to throw some of you into prison, that you may be tested, and you will have tribulation ten days. Be faithful unto death, and I will give you the crown of life' (Revelation 2:10).

I admit that true Christians can grow spiritually cold, surrender to temptation, and commit great sins. Nevertheless, they can never fall away so totally that they get tired of God and obedience, and become settled in a fixed dislike of Christianity. They can never adopt a way of life in which something else is more important than God. They can never entirely lose their distinctness from the unbelieving world, or revert to exactly what they used to be like before their conversion. If this is the effect that problems have on a professing Christian, it shows that he was never truly converted! 'They went out from us, but they were not of us; for if they had been of us, they would have continued with us; but they went out that they might be made manifest, that none of them were of us' (1 John 2:19).

True spiritual emotions, then, always result in Christian practice. Why? I can answer this by reminding you of what we have already seen about the nature of spiritual emotions:

(i) **True spiritual emotions result in Christian practice because they arise from spiritual, supernatural and divine influences on the heart.** No wonder spiritual emotions have such a practical influence, when they have omnipotence on their side! If God dwells in the heart, he will show that he is a God by the power of his operation. Christ is not in the heart of a Christian as a dead Saviour in a tomb, but as a risen and living Saviour in his temple. Spiritual emotions may be less noisy and showy than others, but they have this secret life and power in them, which carry away the heart and make it captive to the will of God.

(ii) **Spiritual emotions result in Christian practice because their object is the loveliness of spiritual things, not our self-interest.** People have a defective Christianity because they are seeking their own interests in it, not God's. So they accept Christianity only to the extent that they think it serves their interests. By contrast, a person who accepts it for its own excellent and lovely nature, accepts everything which has that nature. He embraces Christianity for its own sake, and so he embraces the whole of Christianity. This is why the true Christian practises his faith with perseverance. A person's private interests may after a time clash with Christianity. So a person who accepts Christianity from selfish motives is liable to abandon it from selfish motives. Private interests change, but the spiritual beauty of Christianity never changes. It is stable and always the same.

(iii) **Spiritual emotions result in Christian practice because they are based on the moral excellence of divine things.** No wonder a love of holiness for its own sake inspires a person to practise holiness! Need I say more?

(iv) **Spiritual emotions result in Christian practice because they arise out of spiritual understanding.** Remember, spiritual understanding is a sense of the heart by which a person sees the supreme beauty of divine things. When we see the supreme beauty and glory of Christ, we see that he is worthy of our worship, our obedience, our very lives. This makes us follow him, despite all difficulties. We cannot forget him or exchange him for something else. He has made too deep an impression on us!

(v) **Spiritual emotions result in Christian practice because they bring a conviction of the reality of divine things.** If a person was never fully convinced that there is any reality in Christianity, no wonder he does not take the trouble to practise it a diligent, serious way! No wonder he does not commit himself to a persevering obedience to what might turn out to be unreal! On the other hand, if a person has a full conviction of the reality of divine things, those things will influence his practice more than anything else does. Why? Because of their infinite importance and significance. We cannot fully and sincerely believe in such great things without coming under their controlling influence.

(vi) **Spiritual emotions result in Christian practice because they always exist alongside spiritual humiliation.**

Humility before God inspires obedience, just as pride inspires rebellion. Humility, then, necessarily leads to Christian practice.

(vii) **Spiritual emotions result in Christian practice because they always exist alongside a change of nature.** Men will not thoroughly change their practice unless they have a change of nature. Until the tree is good, the fruit will not be good. If an unconverted person tries to live a Christian life, he is acting against his sinful nature. It is like throwing a stone upwards. Nature finally prevails, and the stone comes down again. However, if we receive a new heavenly nature in Christ, it is natural that we should walk in newness of life, and continue to do so until the end of our days.

(viii) **Spiritual emotions result in Christian practice because they promote a Christlike spirit.** All the qualities I mentioned under this heading — love, humility, peace, forgiveness, compassion — fulfil the second table of God's law (the last six commandments). And this is largely what Christian practice is all about!

(ix) **Spiritual emotions result in Christian practice because they soften the heart and exist alongside a Christian tenderness of spirit.** The softened heart and tender spirit of the true Christian make him painfully sensitive to sin. Obviously this has a profound influence on the way he lives his life.

(x) **Spiritual emotions result in Christian practice because of their beautiful symmetry and balance.** The symmetry and balance of spiritual emotions will produce a corresponding obedience. The Christian will not obey some of God's commands and ignore others. He is determined to be holy in every area of his life, in all circumstances, at all times.

(xi) **Spiritual emotions result in Christian practice because they produce a longing for deeper holiness.** If the reader will look back at chapter 11, he will see that this must obviously be the case. A longing for deeper holiness does not result in a lack of Christian practice!

From all this, it is clear that Christian practice is a distinguishing feature of true conversion. I will go further. Christian practice is the most important of all the marks and signs of conversion, both to the believer himself and to others.

I will devote my next two chapters to this, so that we can have a proper understanding of it.

13.
Christian practice is the chief sign to others of a convert's sincerity.

Christian practice is the chief sign by which we are to judge the sincerity of professing Christians. Scripture is very clear about this. 'You will know them by their fruits' (Matthew 7:16). 'Either make the tree good and its fruit good, or else make the tree bad and its fruit bad; for a tree is known by its fruit' (Matthew 13:33). Christ nowhere says, 'You will know the tree by its leaves and flowers. You will know men by their talk, by the story they tell of their experiences, by their tears and emotional expressions.' No! 'You will know them by their fruits. A tree is known by its fruits.'

Christ tells us to look for the fruit of Christian practice in others. He also tells us that we must show this fruit to others in our own lives. 'Let your light so shine before men, that they may see your good works and glorify your Father in heaven' (Matthew 5:16). Christ does not say, 'Let your light shine by telling others about your feelings and experiences.' It is when others see our good works that they will glorify our Father in heaven.

The rest of the New Testament says the same. For instance, in Hebrews we read about those who were enlightened, tasted the heavenly gift, and so on, and fell away (Hebrews 6:4-8). Then in verse 9 it says: 'But, beloved, we are confident of better things concerning you, yes, things that accompany salvation.' Why was the writer to the Hebrews so confident that **their** faith was real and **they** would not fall away? Because of their Christian practice. See verse 10: 'For God is not unjust to forget your work and labour of love which you have shown towards his name, in that you have ministered to the saints and do minister.'

We find the same teaching in James. 'What does it profit, my brethren, if someone says he has faith but does not have works?' (James 2:14). James is telling us that it is useless to **say** we have faith, if we do not show our faith by good works. Everything we say is worthless, if it is not confirmed by what we do. Personal testimonies, stories about our feelings and experiences — all worthless without good works and Christian practice.

This is really just common sense. Everyone knows that 'actions speak louder than words.' This applies in the spiritual as well as the natural realm. Imagine two people. One seems to walk humbly before God and men, to live a life that speaks of a penitent and contrite heart; he is submissive to God in affliction, meek and gentle towards his fellow men. The other **talks** about how humble he is, how convicted of sin he feels, how he lies in the dust before God, etc. Yet he **behaves** as if he were the head of all the Christians in town! He is bossy, self-important, and cannot stand criticism. Which of these two gives the best evidence of being a real Christian? It is not by telling people about ourselves that we demonstrate our Christianity. Words are cheap. It is by costly, self-denying Christian practice that we show the reality of our faith.

I am assuming, of course, that this Christian practice exists in a person who says he believes the Christian faith. After all, what we are testing is the sincerity of those who claim they are Christians. A person cannot claim to be a Christian without claiming to believe certain things. We would not — and should not — accept as a Christian anyone who denies essential Christian doctrines, no matter how good and holy he seems. Along with Christian practice, there has to be an acceptance of the basic truths of the gospel. These include believing that Jesus is the Messiah, that he died to satisfy God's justice against our sins, and other such doctrines. Christian practice is the best proof of the sincerity and salvation of those who say they believe these truths, but it proves nothing about the salvation of those who deny them!

I would only add what I said earlier (Part Two, chapter 12), that no outward appearances are **infallible** signs of conversion. Christian practice is the **best** evidence we have that a professing Christian is a real Christian. It obliges us to believe in his sincerity and accept him as a brother in Christ. Even so, it is still not one hundred per cent infallible proof. For a start, we cannot see all a person's outward behaviour; much of it is hidden from the world. Nor can we look into a person's heart and see his motives. We cannot be certain how far an unconverted person can go in an outward appearance of Christianity. And yet, if we could see as much of a person's practice as that person's own conscience knows, it might be an infallible sign of his condition. The truth of this will appear in my next chapter.

14. Christian practice is a sure sign of conversion to a person's own conscience.

This is clear from 1 John 2:3, 'By this we know that we know him, if we keep his commandments.' John says we can have assurance of salvation if our consciences testify to our good works: 'My little children, let us not love in word or in tongue, but in deed and in truth. And by this we know that we are of the truth, and shall assure our hearts before him,' 1 John 3:18-19. The apostle Paul tells the Galatians to examine their own behaviour, so that they might rejoice in their salvation: 'let each one examine his own work, and then he will have rejoicing in himself alone, and not in another' (Galatians 6:4). When Christ says, 'By their fruits you will know them' (Matthew 6:20), this is in the first place a rule for judging others; but Christ also wants us to judge ourselves by this rule, as the next verse makes clear: 'Not everyone who says to me, "Lord, Lord," shall enter the kingdom of heaven, but he who does the will of my Father in heaven' (Matthew 6:21).

What exactly does the Bible mean by 'keeping Christ's commandments', 'doing the Father's will', and so on — what we have called Christian practice — when it makes these things the basis of assurance?

Christian practice certainly does not refer merely to outward bodily actions. Obedience is an act of the whole man, soul as well as body. In fact, obedience is really and properly the act of the soul, since the soul governs the body. So Christian practice refers more to the inward obedience of the soul, than to the outward actions of the body.

There are two ways that a Christian's soul can act:

(i) The soul can act in a purely **inward** way which does not result in outward bodily actions. When we simply meditate on God's truth, our minds rest in that truth, and do not go beyond it to some outward act.

(ii) The soul can act in a **practical** way. This results in outward bodily actions. For example, compassion can prompt us to give a cup of cold water to a disciple of Christ (Matthew 10:42), or a person's love for Christ can make him endure all persecutions for Christ's sake. Here is the obedience of the soul exerting itself in bodily actions.

When Scripture makes Christian practice the evidence to others of our faith, it refers to what others can see of our practice — our outward bodily actions. However, when Scripture makes Christian practice the evidence to **ourselves** of our faith, it refers to what **we** can see of our practice — and we can see the inward motives behind our outward actions. So the Christian has to judge his own practice, not just by what he does outwardly with his body, but by the inward motives of his soul which control his bodily actions. This is how God judges us: 'I, the Lord, search the heart, I test the mind, even to give to every man according to his ways, and according to the fruit of his doings' (Jeremiah 17:10). 'And all the churches shall know that I am he who searches the minds and hearts. And I will give to each one of you according to your works' (Revelation 2:23). If God judges us by our outward actions alone, why does he search the minds and the hearts? God is concerned not only about our deeds and works, but about the spirit which lies behind them.

Having said all that, I do not want anyone to think that motives are all that matter, and that what we do outwardly with our bodies is irrelevant. Not at all! We cannot divorce soul and body like that. The soul governs the body. Holy motives produce an obedient lifestyle. So a person who lives an outwardly sinful life cannot make the excuse that his heart is in the right place. A man's heart cannot be pure, and his feet carry him off into a brothel! That is absurd. Christian practice includes both these things — the inward motives and the outward actions. We need to pass the test in both areas. Outwardly good deeds without inwardly holy motives are not Christian practice. Nor are supposedly spiritual motives which do not produce practical bodily obedience.

Christian practice is the best evidence of true faith to the believer's own conscience. We should not place much confidence in religious experiences, convictions, comforts, joys, or those inward meditations which do not result in practical obedience. Let me offer six arguments to show that we must get our assurance mainly from Christian practice:

(i) My first argument is from common sense. The proof that a man prefers something is that he does it. When someone is free to speak or keep silent, the proof that he prefers speaking is that he opens his mouth and speaks. When someone is free to walk or sit still, the proof that he prefers walking is that he gets up and walks. In the same way, the proof that a man prefers obeying God to disobeying him, is that he obeys. So it is absurd for anyone to pretend that he has a good heart while he lives a disobedient life. Is he trying to fool God? The Judge of all the earth will not be mocked with pretences. 'Not everyone who says to me, "Lord, Lord," shall enter the kingdom of heaven, but he who does the will of my Father in heaven. Many will say to me in that day, "Lord, Lord, have we not prophesied in your name, cast our demons in your name, and done many wonders in your name?" And then I will declare to them, "I never knew you; depart from me, you who practise lawlessness!"' (Matthew 7:21-3). No matter how many religious experiences we have, even if we work miracles, we cannot hide a disobedient life from our Judge. We will not be able to impress him or fool him with any excuses. After all, not even a human master would put up with a servant who professed great love and loyalty to his master, but refused to obey him!

(ii) My second argument is from God's providence. God sends problems and tests into our lives, to see whether in practice we will prefer him to other things. We find ourselves in a situation where God is on one side, and something else is on the other — and we cannot have both. We must choose. Our practical choices in these situations show whether we love God supremely or not. 'And you shall remember that the Lord your God led you all the way those forty years in the wilderness, to humble you and test you, to know what was in your heart, whether you would keep his commandments or not' (Deuteronomy 8:2).

These tests are for our benefit, not God's. He already knows what is in our hearts. He brings us into testing situations so that **we** might know what is in our hearts. God is educating us, not himself! Given that this is the way God teaches us about our hearts, it proves that our practice is the true evidence of our sincerity.

(iii) Christian practice brings the new birth to perfection. James says that Abraham's practical obedience perfected his faith: 'Do you see that faith was working together with his works, and by works faith was made perfect?' (James 2:22). John says that our practical obedience perfects our love for God: 'He who says, "I know him," and does not keep his commandments, is a liar, and the truth is not in him. But whoever keeps his word, truly the love of God is perfected in him' (1 John 2:4-5).

So Christian practice perfects faith and love. They are like a seed. A seed does not come to perfection by being planted in the earth. Nor does it come to perfection by putting forth root and shoot, nor by coming out of the ground, nor by growing leaves and blossoms. However, when it produces good ripe fruit, it has come to perfection — it has fulfilled its nature. It is the same with faith and love and all other graces. They come to perfection in the good ripe fruits of Christian practice. Practice, then, must be the best evidence that these graces exist.

(iv) Scripture emphasises practice more than any other evidence of salvation. I hope this is clear by now. We have to keep to this emphasis. It is dangerous to lay stress on things which the Bible does not. We have lost our Biblical balance if we major on feelings and experiences which do not express themselves in practical obedience. God knows what is best for us, and he has underlined certain things because they need underlining. If we ignore God's clear emphasis on Christian practice, and stress other things as tests of sincerity, we are on the way to delusion and hypocrisy.

(v) Scripture speaks very **clearly** about Christian practice as the true test of sincerity. It is not as if this were some obscure doctrine, mentioned only a few times in difficult passages. Suppose God gave a new revelation today, and declared, 'You shall know my disciples by this, you shall know that you are of the truth by this, you can know that you know me by this' — and then gave a special mark or sign. Would we not look on this as a clear, emphatic test of sincerity and salvation? Well, this is what has happened! God **has** spoken from heaven — in the Bible! He has again and again told us that Christian practice is the highest and best proof of real faith. See how Christ repeats this test over and over again in chapter 14 of John's gospel: 'If you love me, keep my commandments' (v. 15). 'He who has my commandments and keeps them, it is he who loves me' (v. 21). 'If anyone loves me, he will keep my word' (v. 23). 'He who does not love me does not keep my word' (v. 24). And in chapter 15: 'By this my Father is glorified, that you bear much fruit; so shall you be my disciples' (v. 8). 'You are my friends if you do whatever I command you' (v. 14). And we find the same in 1 John: 'Now by this we know that we know him, if we keep his commandments' (2:3). 'Whoever keeps his word, truly the love of God is perfected in him. By this we know that we are in him' (2:5). 'Let us not love in word or in tongue, but in deed and in truth. By this we know that we are of the truth' (3:18-19).

Is this unclear?

(vi) God will judge us by our practice on Judgment Day. He will not ask us to give our personal testimony. He will not examine our religious experiences. The evidence on which the Judge will accept or reject us will be our practice. This evidence, of course, will not be for God's benefit. He knows our hearts. Even so, he will display the evidence of our practice because of the open, public nature of his final judgment. 'For we must all appear before the judgment seat of Christ, that each one may receive the things done in the body, according to what he has done, whether good or bad' (2 Corinthians 5:10). If our practice is the decisive evidence God will use on Judgment

Day, that is the test we ought to apply ourselves here and now.

From these arguments, I think it is clear that Christian practice (as I have defined it) is the best evidence, to ourselves and others, that we are true Christians.

Of course, when someone has only just been converted, he has had no opportunity to practise a holy life. He may have an assurance of salvation based purely on his inward emotions and experience. That does not alter the fact that the **best** and **most solid** evidence of a person's salvation is when his emotions and his experience express themselves in a life of practical obedience. A man may be willing to go on a dangerous journey to a far country. He may be sure that he is prepared for all the hardship and sacrifice he must endure. Still, the best proof, to himself and to others, that he really is willing and prepared for this journey, is **that he goes.**

There are two main objections people will raise to what I have said.

The first objection is that spiritual experience rather than practice is the real proof that we are Christians. This is a misunderstanding of what I have said. To speak of spiritual experience and Christian practice as if they were two separate things is completely wrong. Christian practice is spiritual practice. It is not a body acting mindlessly. It is the action of soul and body together, the soul moving and governing the body. So Christian practice does not exclude spiritual experience. We would not practise true obedience at all, without the spiritual acts of the soul. The emotion of love for God is not an unspiritual experience just because it shows itself in an outward act of self-denial!

There is an outward religious practice without inward experience. That is good for nothing. However, there is also religious experience without practice, without Christian behaviour. That is worse than nothing! True religious experience is where we love God, and our love makes us choose him, and obey him, and stand by him in all difficult and testing situations.

Friendship between human beings consists mainly in an inward affection; but when their affection actually carries them through fire and water for each other — that is the highest proof of friendship.

The second objection is that my emphasis on practice is legalistic — it concentrates too much on works, and so will lead people away from the great gospel doctrine of justification by faith alone.

This is nonsense. I have not said that our practice is the **price** of God's favour. I have said that it is the **sign** of God's favour. If I gave a beggar some money, and the beggar looked on the money as a sign of my love for him, would that destroy the freeness of my love? Of course not. Nor does it destroy the freeness of God's love to us, if we look on the obedience he creates in us as a sign of his love.

The doctrine of God's free grace to sinners means that there are no good qualities in us which can earn or deserve his grace. God loves His elect freely and sovereignly, out of the infinite riches of his own divine nature, and not because of anything beautiful in the elect. Similarly, justification without works means that no lovely quality or action in us can ever atone for our sins. God accepts us as righteous because of Christ's obedience, not our own. And when Scripture contrasts faith with works, it means that sinners are not united to Christ because of the beauty or the goodness of their works, or their feelings, or of anything else in them. In fact, it is not even the beauty or goodness of our faith which unites us to Christ! Faith joins us to the Saviour quite apart from any goodness or beauty it may have. Why? Simply because faith **means** receiving, accepting and resting on Jesus with our souls.

Let us be very clear about this. It **would** destroy the freeness of God's grace if the loveliness and excellence of anything at all in us joined us to Christ. Love for God, spiritual joy, self-denial, experiences, feelings, works — no matter how good any of these things are, their goodness does not unite us to

Christ. Nowhere have I taught that! I have taught that these things are **signs** of our union with Christ. They show that we **are** united to him by faith alone.

To have a casual attitude to good works because they do not justify us, is really no different from being casual about all obedience, all holiness, all spiritual mindedness — because they do not justify us either! Yet what Christian will say that a zeal for obedience, holiness and spiritual mindedness is inconsistent with justification by faith? Holy practice is the sign of faith, just as activity and movement are the signs of life.

15.
Conclusion.

What a lot of trouble the Church would have escaped, if Christians had kept to what Scripture teaches about a true experience of salvation! Scripture tells us to judge ourselves and others in this area mainly by the fruit of practical Christian obedience. If only we kept to this, it would expose hypocrisy and self-deception more powerfully than anything else could. It would rescue us from the endless confusion caused by man-made theories about what we ought to be experiencing. It would prevent Christians from neglecting holiness of life. It would encourage them to show their Christianity by the beauty of their conduct, rather than by constantly declaring their experiences. Christian friends would talk together of their experiences in a more modest and humble way, seeking to edify rather than to impress one another. Many opportunities of spiritual pride would be cut off, to the frustration of the devil. Worldly people would cease to laugh at or scorn Christianity because of the follies of Christians; instead, unbelievers would become convinced that there is reality in Christianity, and would pay attention to its claims, when they saw the lives of believers.

And so the light of Christians would shine before men, and others would see their good works and glorify their Father in heaven!